# JUDICIAL REVIEW
# OF LEGISLATION

Da Capo Press Reprints in

## AMERICAN CONSTITUTIONAL AND LEGAL HISTORY

GENERAL EDITOR: LEONARD W. LEVY

*Claremont Graduate School*

# JUDICIAL REVIEW
# OF LEGISLATION

## By Robert von Moschzisker

DA CAPO PRESS · NEW YORK · 1971

A Da Capo Press Reprint Edition

This Da Capo Press edition of *Judicial Review of Legislation* is an unabridged republication of the first edition published by the National Association for Constitutional Government, Washington, D.C., in 1923.

Library of Congress Catalog Card Number 78-153372
SBN 306-70151-0

Published by Da Capo Press, Inc.
A Subsidiary of Plenum Publishing Corporation
227 West 17th Street, New York, N.Y. 10011
All Rights Reserved

Manufactured in the United States of America

# JUDICIAL REVIEW
# OF LEGISLATION

# JUDICIAL REVIEW OF LEGISLATION

A CONSIDERATION OF THE WARRANTS FOR
AND MERITS OF OUR AMERICAN SYSTEM OF
JUDICIALLY REVIEWING LEGISLATION TO
ASCERTAIN ITS CONSTITUTIONAL VALIDITY

---

By **ROBERT** von **MOSCHZISKER, LL. D.**
CHIEF JUSTICE OF PENNSYLVANIA

# PREFACE

THESE two lectures, delivered before the Law School of the University of Pennsylvania, were prepared with the thought of helping to dispel a popular misconception concerning the origin of the power of the American judiciary to determine the constitutionality of legislation, also in the hope of demonstrating the falsity of various teachings antagonistic to the right of judicial review, and of counteracting the effect of current attacks, launched from many quarters, against the system which has grown up under this now well-established doctrine.

For the historical data employed, I am largely indebted to other writers (mentioned in the text and footnotes) who have treated of that phase of the subject, but not so succinctly as here undertaken; my own contribution in this regard consists of an effort to marshal the essential facts in the briefest form compatible with their adequate presentation, and yet in a manner calculated to attract the average person. The first lecture is chiefly given over to this endeavor, while the second contains thoughts on the proper conclusions to be drawn from the historic facts previously detailed, discussion of the merits of the doctrine of judicial review, consideration of the recent attacks on the power of the courts to declare legislation invalid and pending suggestions for the limitation of that power. The second lecture also contains some freshly gathered statistics which, with their tabulation in the addenda, should be informing.

For undertaking the circulation of these lectures among a wider audience than they might otherwise reach, I am under obligation to the National Association for Constitutional Government. To Mr. Henry Campbell Black, the Editor of the Constitutional Review, and to Mr. Henry E. Randall, Editor in Chief of the West Publishing Company, I am indebted for the expression of their valued opinions that the dissemination of my work would prove of public service, and for their general and very practical interest in the matter of the present publication.

ROBERT VON MOSCHZISKER.

PHILADELPHIA, PA.,
June, 1923.

# TABLE OF CONTENTS

# FIRST LECTURE

## I.  INTRODUCTION

IN discussing the subject of these lectures,—the power exercised by American courts to review legislation for the purpose of determining its constitutionality,—I shall deal, from historical and other standpoints, with what is commonly called the doctrine of judicial review, to show (1) that the system developed from this doctrine does not represent a usurpation of power, as is so often charged; (2) that the power in question was intended by the founders of our country; and (3) that it has justified itself through successful operation.  Then I shall advance arguments to prove the system better than any other suggested substitute; but, before entering on these, the principal aspects of my theme, it may be well to call attention to a few relevant preliminary

1                   [1]

considerations, and to note, incidentally, why the matter of judicial review commands attention at this particular time.

To begin with, practically every one agrees that effective government under a written constitution requires the recognition of some agency as vested with power to determine the meaning of the organic law, and it is generally conceded that, so far as conflicts between acts of state legislatures and the federal Constitution are concerned, the latter, by clear implication, makes it the duty of the courts, if such legislation is properly challenged before them, to determine whether it conflicts with the organic law.[1] There have always been a few, however, who contend against this judicial power as applied to federal statutes, arguing that Congress, when legislating, possesses an absolute right to interpret the Constitution, and that there is no evidence, in that instrument or elsewhere, of an intention that such legislative inter-

[1] See dissenting opinion of Gibson, J., in Eakin v. Raub. 12 Serg. & R. (Pa.) 330, 345, 355–357.

pretations should be open to attack in the courts. A like argument would lie against the right of state courts to review state legislation, where that power is not expressly granted by the local Constitution.

How this idea of the infallibility of the legislature can be made to work effectively in the everyday affairs of the people it is difficult to see, if we stop to consider that constitutional questions customarily appear, not by looking at a suggested piece of legislation in an abstract or academic way, to ascertain whether it agrees or conflicts with the fundamental law, but when, in some real affair of life, it becomes necessary to apply actual legislation to circumstances affecting a given individual or situation. Then, if occasion requires, the courts examine both the Constitution and the legislation, in order to determine their respective meanings, and it is only in this incidental way that acts are found to be unconstitutional.

The principle is now well established that no person can attack an act of the legislature on the ground of unconstitutionality, unless actually affecting him in the particular transaction under investigation, and, when such an attack is properly made, should the court find the legislation to conflict with the Constitution, it does not, theoretically, annul the act, but simply ascertains the fact of the conflict, and, if the difference is material and irreconcilable, since the Constitution must prevail as the superior rule of action, the statute, or the challenged part, necessarily falls of its own weight,[2] at least as applicable to that case; the judicial announcement of invalidity serving merely as formal binding notice, which in practice is understood to rule similar states of fact, though such announcements are generally accepted as disposing of the question of the invalidity of the legislation for all future purposes, if the scope of the decision warrants it.

The right of the courts to pronounce

---

[2] Miller v. Belmont Packing & Rubber Co., 268 Pa. 51, 62, 110 Atl. 802.

legislation void, when an irreconcilable conflict between a statute and the Constitution develops in the manner just indicated, is, I am convinced, firmly and wisely imbedded in the fabric of our government; but there are many who think otherwise. This is apparent when we realize that a United States senator [3] recently expressed an intention to introduce, in the near future, a constitutional amendment which would deprive the federal Supreme Court of its present power to decide conclusively as to conflicts between acts of Congress and the Constitution,—a power which he, for one, thinks unwarranted by our organic law. The proposal in question has received the indorsement of no less a body than the American Federation of Labor, [4] indicating that possibly many others agree with this senator's thought. A second eminent senator [5] has suggested an act of

[3] Senator La Follette, on June 21, 1922, Congressional Record, vol. 62, No. 160, pp. 9851, 9857.
[4] See minutes of the A. F. of L. Convention, held at Cincinnati, June 22, 1922.
[5] Senator Borah, of Idaho.

Congress to regulate the exercise of the right of review, and another proposal along the same line, though somewhat less radical, is made by a third senator.[6]

The suggested changes (each of which I shall discuss more fully later on) have evoked much editorial comment both favorable and unfavorable,[7] wherein it is repeatedly asserted that the idea of the right of the federal courts to review legislation sprang full-grown from the mind of John Marshall; and the omnipotence of the English Parliament is often pointed to as an example for us to follow,—also as indicating a system known to our ancestors which they probably intended to continue. Consideration will, I am convinced, show all of these contentions unwarranted.

A nation usually develops the governmental system best suited to its temperament. The Englishman holds fast to that which is established by custom, while the

---

[6] Senator Fess, of Ohio.

[7] Various views taken are set forth in the Literary Digest for July 1, 1922, at page 21, and see current newspapers.

American is inclined to bury the past each day at midnight and start all over again the next morning—a national tendency which must be kept in mind as a material consideration whenever we contemplate the possibility of a departure from our present system of judicially checking up acts of the legislature by comparing them with the written fundamental law, which the people originally agreed among themselves should be obeyed by all, including their representatives in the legislature.

Whether or not our system is ideal in theory, it has lasted so long now that, as a matter of fact, the American legislator devotes himself in the main to questions of policy and expediency, leaving those of conflicts of law to the experts in the courts, who, to that end, are equally the representatives of the people,—representatives specially fitted for the purpose in view, and, we may fairly assume, far more equal to the task thus imposed than our legislative bodies are, or could possibly be made through any change of system.

There have always been those who contend that judicial review of federal legislation by the national courts finds no warrant in the letter, the spirit, or the history of the Constitution,[8] though the large ma-

---

[8] Gibson's dissenting opinion in Eakin v. Raub, 12 Serg. & R. (Pa.) 330, 339.

Allan L. Benson, "The Usurped Power of the Courts"; "Our Dishonest Constitution."

Louis B. Boudin, "Government by Judiciary," 26 Pol. Science Quart. 238.

Walter Clark, C. J., of North Carolina, address of April 27, 1906, reprinted in Congressional Record, July 31, 1911; address of Jan. 27, 1914, "Government by Judges," published Senate Doc. 610, U. S. 63d Congress, 2d Sess.

Horace A. Davis, "Annulment of Legislation by the Supreme Court," 7 Am. Pol. Sc. Rev. 541–587.

Wm. J. Gaynor, "Our Courts and Social Progress," 28 Bench & Bar, 1912, pp. 102–106.

Senator Robert M. La Follette, Address of June 14, 1922, Congressional Record, vol. 62, No. 160, pp. 9851–9858.

Senator Robert L. Owen, Congressional Record, July 31, 1911, vol. 47, pp. 3367, 3368.

Jackson H. Ralston, "Judicial Control over Legislation," 54 Am. Law Rev. 1–38, 193–230.

Gilbert E. Roe, "Our Judicial Oligarchy," La Follette's Weekly Magazine, vol. III, No. 25, pp. 7–9.

Dean William Trickett, "The Great Usurpation," 40 Am. Law Rev. 356–376; "Judicial Dispensation from Congressional Statutes," 41 Am. Law Rev. 65; and "Judicial Nullification of Acts of Congress," North Am. Rev. vol. 185, p. 848.

jority of writers, statesmen, and judges, who have studied the evidence, do not agree with this opinion. Nevertheless, since the minority,—and, I think, mistaken, —idea now finds formidable advocates, it calls for renewed and serious consideration. It is not my purpose, however, to discuss the right of review from a strictly legal aspect, because the point of law that the courts possess this power is firmly established by many well-considered judicial decisions, some of which will be incidentally mentioned as we proceed.

The general questions which I shall discuss may be stated thus: First, whether there are any early precedents which support the right of the courts, as now exercised, to determine finally what the fundamental law is and whether particular legislation conflicts therewith; second, and especially, whether the right to exercise this power was, in point of fact, intended to be conferred on the courts by those who framed and adopted our Constitution: third, the real character, and merits, of the doctrine which supports the right of judicial review and of the system which it has developed; and, finally, the weaknesses and dangers of the proposed substitutes.

## II.  ANCIENT PRECEDENTS

Long before America was discovered, there existed in Europe certain unwritten systems of law by which, at times, legislation was judicially determined to be void because contrary to a paramount law.[9]  It is not at all probable that our plan of government is in any respect a conscious imitation of a Grecian pattern; but it is interesting to note that, in the political system of the early Greek democracies (508–338 B. C.), as described by Viscount Bryce,[10] we find a form of judicial review which, in principle, so closely resembles the American doctrine as to deserve mention here.

The population of these early democra-

---

[9] Brinton Coxe, "Judicial Power and Unconstitutional Legislation," p. 45.

[10] James Bryce, "Modern Democracies," vol. 1, pp. 194–200.

cies was usually less than ten thousand; even Athens, to which I shall confine my present observations, had only thirty thousand. Such conditions enabled the whole body of citizens to meet together for political purposes, and rendered practicable a government by the people in the strictest sense,—the Athenian Assembly, or body of the citizens, being vested with executive, legislative, and judicial powers.

The Athenians "drew a distinction between *laws,* containing general rules of permanent operation, and *decrees,* passed for a particular occasion and purpose." Amendment of the laws was effected at special times by proposals, which were drafted in final form, after acceptance by the Assembly, and passed by a special body of five hundred or more citizens (the Thesmothetai), chosen by lot. "To protect the laws from infringement by the Assembly,—that is to say, to protect the citizens from their own hasty or ignorant action,— a check was contrived: Whoever brought forth and carried in the Assembly a decree which transgressed any law, in form or substance, might be prosecuted" criminally, and the illegal decree annulled. This prosecution, punishment of the transgressor, and annulment of the decree, necessitated judicial action by the citizens, and for that purpose they were organized into another special body (called the Heliæa), consisting of all who offered themselves to take the judicial oath. Although this Assembly might sit as a whole, it usually acted by groups of about five hundred (known as Dikasteries), to one of which every case, civil or criminal, was referred. In this way the Athenians acted judicially, and frequently set aside, as repugnant to the fundamental laws, decrees which they themselves had promulgated when acting legislatively. In the United States, to-day, when our courts determine a statute to be in conflict with the fundamental law, they are, as agents, performing an act which these Athenians, in a pure democracy, accomplished directly.

In his book, entitled "Judicial Power

and Unconstitutional Legislation," Mr. Brinton Coxe sets forth[11] other early precedents for judicial review, to be found in the Roman law and in the French public law long before the Revolution of 1787, as well as in the canon-law doctrine, prevailing both on the continent and in England before 1688, which enabled the ecclesiastical courts to nullify temporal statutes. While these analogies of antiquity are interesting, I do not of course claim them as the source of our modern doctrine; for this we must look to later times and different places.

## III.  ORIGIN OF AMERICAN DOCTRINE

There was a Roman and medieval conception of a supreme law of nature, ordained by God and taking precedence over temporal laws in conflict with it; and this idea of certain fundamental principles controlling government finds noteworthy ex-

---

[11] Pages 83, 105-164.

pression in Magna Charta.[12] Not until the seventeenth century, however, do we find any persistent attempt to assert the right of judges to interpret this so-called fundamental, paramount law in the face of executive or legislative action; then Sir Edward Coke ventured to challenge the royal prerogative, and to inform James I there were certain underlying rules not even he could alter. "Magna Charta," said the Chief Justice, "is such a fellow that he will have no sovereign."[13] At this time Coke dreamed of making the common-law courts superior to both King and Parliament; though subsequently he seemed to realize that the latter, as the highest court of the realm, must have an ultimate right to interpret the fundamental law.[14] With

---

[12] E. S. Corwin, "The Doctrine of Judicial Review," p. 27, citing C. H. McIlwain, "The High Court of Parliament and Its Supremacy" (1911), and G. B. Adams, "The Origin of the English Constitution" (1912).

[13] The contest between James I and Coke is fully set forth in Gardiner's History of England, 1603–1642, vols. 2, 3.

[14] Corwin, "The Doctrine of Judicial Review," pp. 29, 68.

the English Revolution of 1688 came the established supremacy of Parliament, resulting in the disappearance of references to fundamental law, and, for the time being, reducing Coke's theories of common-law superiority to a heap of smouldering dicta, not to be fanned into flame till pre-Revolutionary days in America, a fact I shall refer to later and more at length; but it is important to note at this point that, historically, the triumph of Parliament over the King was due to its judicial rather than its legislative functions, and it was recognition of the actual existence of both these powers in the same body which really caused discussion of the subject of the fundamental law to disappear in England.

Keeping in mind this double power, which is vested in Parliament, it becomes amazingly simple, says Mr. Herbert Pope in the Harvard Law Review,[15] to reconcile the enforcement of the fundamental law in England and in America. In each country, the highest judicial tribunal is

---

[15] 27 Harvard Law Rev. 59–61.

the ultimate interpreter of the fundamental law, whether it be written or unwritten. The difference is that, with us,—
where the legislative and judicial functions
are vested in distinct and separate bodies,—
there must necessarily result the right of
the judiciary, whose sole function it is to
interpret and enforce the law, to hold void
legislative acts inconsistent with the provisions of the Constitution; whereas, in
England, historically the promulgation of a
legislative act was ipso facto a declaration
by the highest court (i. e., The House of
Lords) that the act did not transgress the
fundamental law. The distinction between
the American and English systems is of importance, for, considering our constitutional
separation of governmental powers, the
right of the judiciary to protect the Constitution from legislative impairment seems
inescapably essential to the maintenance of
our written fundamental law; and it is my
purpose to show that the exercise of this
power can reasonably be looked upon as

intended by those who wrote and adopted the Constitution.

## IV. DEVELOPMENT OF THE DOCTRINE IN COLONIAL TIMES

No grant, in precise words, of the power of judicial review over acts of Congress, is made in the federal Constitution; but I think the right is sufficiently expressed, and agree with Professor Corwin [16] that it rests on "general principles which, in the estimation of the framers made [more] specific provision for it unnecessary." The implication of such power, from provisions of the Constitution which I shall mention in due course, is irresistible. A proper understanding of the principles in question, which are evidenced by the provisions to be considered and the whole structure of the Constitution, necessitates a glimpse into the historic background wherein the doctrine,—that it is the duty of the courts, when administering the law,

---

[16] Corwin, "The Doctrine of Judicial Review," p. 17.

2         [ 17 ]

to guard the Constitution and give litigants the paramount rights which it guarantees,—slowly grew to its present stable position. With this end in mind, we shall examine certain relevant data, including various colonial and state precedents, opinions of the framers, and views expressed in the ratifying conventions.

The first of numerous influences worthy of note may be found in our political system before the Revolution, particularly as it centered around the right of review over colonial legislation possessed and exercised by the Privy Council of England. As we all know, the colonies were governed under royal charters, or letters patent, subject to supervision or review, Professor Thayer states, "by forfeiture of the charters by act of Parliament, by the direct annulling of legislation by the Crown, [or] by judicial proceedings and an ultimate appeal to the Privy Council." [17] The acts of assembly of nine of the thirteen col-

---

[17] Thayer, "Origin and Scope of the American Doctrine of Constitutional Law." in "Legal Essays," p. 3.

onies, during at least some period of their existence, had to be submitted to the King in Council, where they were subject to disapproval and repeal; and, in addition to this right of reviewing provincial acts directly, the Privy Council had power to hear cases "appealed home" from colonial courts. Mr. Douglas W. Brown, in an interesting and carefully prepared address delivered on November 16, 1922, before the West Virginia Bar Association, of which he was president, states:

"On the ground that they conflicted with the colonial charter or with the laws of England, acts of the colonial legislatures were disallowed from Virginia in 1677, from Rhode Island in 1704, from Connecticut in 1705, from North Carolina in 1747, from Pennsylvania in 1760, from New Hampshire in 1764, and from Massachusetts in 1772. In all, 8,563 acts of the colonies, which later formed the United States, were submitted to the Privy Council, of which 469 were disallowed, a large proportion of them upon the ground of

lack of authority on the part of the legislatures to enact them. In addition to appeals to the Privy Council from the enactments of colonial legislatures, there were
also many appeals from the decisions of
colonial courts."

The most famous of the colonial appeal
cases, Winthrop v. Lechmere,[18] related to
the validity of an act of the Connecticut
assembly abolishing primogeniture. The
Privy Council reversed the judgment of
the Superior Court of Connecticut, and
held the act "null and void," saying it was
"contrary to the law of this realm, unrea-
sonable, and against the tenor of their
charter,"—adding, "consequently the province had no power to make such a law."
Whether the annulment of legislative acts,
in this and similar cases appealed from a
lower court, was theoretically an exercise
by the Privy Council of legislative or judicial power, is a mooted question,[19] which

---

[18] Thayer, "Cases on Constitutional Law," vol. 1, p. 34.
[19] Coxe thinks this power legislative. See his "Judicial Power," p. 212; Thayer thinks it judicial. See
"Cases on Constitutional Law," pp. 39, 40.

matters little for our present purpose, since, in either event, the fact remains that, in the course of what originated as a judicial proceeding, the ultimate tribunal declared acts of assembly void. Even though the reviewing authority was the restraining hand of a superior government placed on the acts of its inferior, and therefore lacked the element of review of the legality of legislation by a co-ordinate branch of government,— that element being part of our present consideration,—nevertheless the practice then pursued served to acquaint the colonists with the custom of having legislative acts pronounced void by another governmental body, and from that standpoint it has an important bearing on our study.

Mr. William M. Meigs, in his excellent little book, "The Judiciary and the Constitution," very plausibly suggests that the power of the colonial assemblies to fix the salaries of the judges may have deprived the latter of their freedom of action, and made them "slow to decide that laws passed by their actual master were void because of being in violation of some law or charter which owed its force to a power on the other side of tempestuous seas, three thousand miles away,—a distance then of long, long months, or even of years," [20] and this may account for the dearth of such cases,—or perhaps a diligent search through dusty files of bygone days would reveal them.

Mr. Meigs gives us, however, one instance tending to show that, if the colonial courts did not frequently exercise the power of review, at least the doctrine was not unknown to them. In 1697 Massachusetts passed an act regulating the values of foreign coins, and in due course this was approved by the Privy Council; in 1704 Parliament enacted legislation of its own regulating such values, and there was already existing another act by which all colonial statutes at variance with acts of Parliament were to be treated as void.[21] Between these conflicting enactments the co-

[20] Meigs, "The Judiciary and the Constitution," p. 37.
[21] Statutes of the Realm, VII, p. 105.

lonial courts had to choose, and we are told by the then Governor of Massachusetts that, "after the passing of the act of Parliament, the provincial courts, at least, appear to have followed the values prescribed therein." [22] This, in effect, was an instance of the judicial denial by a provincial court of the binding force, or validity, of a colonial legislative act; but we do not find the doctrine of the right of judicial review broadly asserted till the period of the Revolution. Discussion of the subject of a higher law controlling legislative acts had been before the public in one form or another for some time, and, culminating as this discussion did on the eve of the Revolution, it must have left an indelible impression on the minds of our ancestors.

James Otis crystallized political thought on the theory of a fundamental law binding kings and legislators; in fact, it was largely through his brilliant and passionate appeals that the colonists early learned the philoso-

---

[22] Meigs, "The Judiciary and the Constitution," pp. 45–47.

phy which was to justify the Revolution and form the basis of the present American system of judicial review.

Difficulties met by British officials in enforcing various stamp acts led Parliament to authorize colonial courts to issue "writs of assistance," enabling the officers of the crown to make house to house searches in their efforts to detect smuggling. Otis, opposing the issuance of these warrants by a Massachusetts tribunal, declared the existence of a fundamental law which knew no master, saying that, if Parliament transgressed it, the courts should not follow such legislation.[23] Several years later (1764), in a pamphlet entitled "The Rights of the British Colonies Asserted and Proved," [24] Otis set forth an argument of enormous influence in convincing the colonists that, as Englishmen, they possessed certain inalienable rights which had been challenged

---

[23] Otis quoted from Viner. See Quincy Reports (Mass.) 474.

[24] See essay on the "Power to Hold Laws Unconstitutional," in Prof. Andrew C. McLaughlin's "The Courts, the Constitution, and Parties."

by the recent enactment of Parliament. "The supreme legislature," he said, "cannot justly assume power of ruling by extempore arbitrary decrees, but is bound to dispense justice by known settled rules, and by duly authorized independent judges.[25] * * * These are their bounds, which by God and nature are fixed; hitherto have they a right to come, and no further. * * * These are the first principles of law and justice, and the great barriers of a free state, and of the British constitution in particular. To say that Parliament is absolute and arbitrary is a contradiction. The Parliament cannot make two and two five; omnipotency cannot do it. The supreme power in a state is jus dicere only; jus dare, strictly speaking, belongs alone to God. Should an act of Parliament be against any of His natural laws, which are immutably true, their declaration would be contrary to eternal truth, equity, and justice, and consequently void;

---

[25] James Otis, "The Rights of the British Colonies Asserted and Proved," p. 55.

and so it would be adjudged by the Parliament itself when convinced of their mistake. * * * When such mistake is evident and palpable, * * * the judges of the executive courts have declared the act 'of a whole Parliament void.' " [26]

These doctrines of Otis were voiced by other contemporary leaders, such as John and Samuel Adams, and we find them reflected in debates of colonial assemblies and records of town meetings, at various times and places during the decade preceding 1776.[27] Otis' theory of a fundamental law had been taken from Coke's oft-quoted dictum in Dr. Bonham's Case,[28] where it was said that "when an act of parliament is against common right and reason, or repugnant or impossible to be performed, the common law will control it, and adjudge such act to be void." Lord Hobart and Lord Holt had also written

---

[26] Id., p. 70.

[27] See Report of Committee of N. Y. State Bar Ass'n, 1915, pp. 242–258; also Thayer, "Cases on Constitutional Law," p. 52, and note.

[28] 8 Coke Reports, 107, 118 (1612).

obiter to the same effect. Whatever may have been the meaning such dicta were intended to convey,[29] we have it on very high authority [30] that there is no recorded instance "in which an English court of justice has openly taken upon itself to overrule or disregard the plain meaning of an act of Parliament"; but the American lawyers of Revolutionary days were thoroughly familiar with the Institutes of Lord Coke, and so, when the yoke bore too heavily on them and their fellow colonists, they were content to find in his words, and the words of other famous English judges, statements on which they might base the rights they had determined to vindicate,— whether these opinions found legal basis in recorded English decisions was a matter of little moment to them, as it is to us, for the important fact is that the leaders of

[29] See Corwin, "The Doctrine of Judicial Review," p. 68.

[30] Prof. Pollock, in his "First Book of Jurisprudence," p. 264. This view is supported by other writers. See C. G. Haines, "The American Doctrine of Judicial Supremacy," p. 33.

American thought then believed in and proclaimed the doctrine of Coke. While this doctrine,—that, for all Englishmen, there is a fundamental law which not even Parliament in its pretended omnipotence can take away,—made a strong appeal, the other side of the question was also discussed. Blackstone's Commentaries had been sold largely in the Colonies before the Revolution,[31] and from this source American lawyers became familiar with the notion of legislative sovereignty. I think we may say that the net results of the discussions were that the people came more and more to look with favor on the theory of the existence of a fundamental law, and to view an uncontrolled legislature as dangerous to individual liberty. Thus, as confidence in the courts increased, the sentiment was ripe for the acceptance of the idea of judicial review.

---

[31] Kent tells us 2,500 copies were sold. See Corwin, "The Doctrine of Judicial Review," p. 33; but see list of only 840 subscribers preceding the title page of the fourth book of Blackstone's Commentaries, published at Philadelphia by Robert Bell in 1772.

When the ties between ourselves and the mother country were finally cut, Montesquieu's doctrine of separation of the powers of government found favor, and was embodied in a majority of the early state constitutions. This was first applied as a check, not so much on the legislature as on the executive,[32] for colonial experience had shown that governors were more to be feared than popular assemblies. Nevertheless, familiarity with the doctrine, during "the critical period," taught the colonists to look upon the legislative and judicial departments as exercising distinct powers, and accustomed every one to an attitude of judicial independence,—an important factor in the development of our present system.[33]

Another idea that became prevalent during the formative period of the nation was the conception of a written constitution as defining the fundamental law,

---

[32] Corwin "The Doctrine of Judicial Review," p. 35.

[33] This idea is very fully and clearly set forth by Prof. McLaughlin at page 50 of his book, "The Courts, the Constitution, and Parties."

which limited the powers of every branch of government, and this conception furnished the legal basis for state courts checking their legislatures when the latter's enactments showed clear violations of the fundamental law. Many such instances of judicial review may be pointed to, antedating the national Constitutional Convention of 1787.

## V. STATE PRECEDENTS FOR JUDICIAL REVIEW [34]

The New Jersey case of Holmes v. Walton, decided in 1780,[35] is the first reported instance of a state court refusing to follow an act of its Legislature. This case in-

---

[34] The cases discussed in this section are given full consideration by Prof. Haines in his "American Doctrine of Judicial Supremacy," pp. 74–95. It seems that the weight of authority is not in favor of attaching much importance to the case of Josiah Phillips, which is cited as the first state precedent by Prof. Haines. See Meigs, "The Judiciary and the Constitution," p. 60, and authorities there cited.

[35] For a detailed discussion of the case and its significance, see Prof. Austin W. Scott's "Holmes v. Walton, the New Jersey Precedent," Rutgers College Publications, No. 8.

volved the enforcement of a war measure, which provided for trial by a jury of six, without appeal, of persons found with goods of the enemy in their possession. The state Constitution stipulated that "the inestimable right of trial by jury shall remain confirmed as a part of the law of this colony, without repeal, forever." Although the opinion is not recorded, undisputed evidence shows that the act was held void as violative of this constitutional provision. Various petitions were presented to the legislature, complaining because "the Supreme Court has set aside some of the laws as unconstitutional;" but the legislature acquiesced in the judicial finding by passing another law requiring a jury of twelve, if demanded by either party. Several members of the federal Convention of 1787 were intimately associated with the trial of this case: David Brearly, as Chief Justice; William Paterson, as Attorney General; and William Livingston, as Governor and Chancellor of New Jersey.

Five years afterwards, Gouverneur Morris, of Pennsylvania, in referring to the decision, showed the lasting impression of Holmes v. Walton, and his words also reflect the sentiment against legislative sovereignty which was then steadily growing. "They know," said Morris, "that the boasted omnipotence of legislative authority is but a jingle of words. * * * Whatever interpretation lawyers may give, freemen must feel it to be absurd and unconstitutional. Absurd, because laws cannot alter the nature of things; unconstitutional, because the constitution is no more, if it can be changed by the legislature." While Morris thus denied the supremacy of the legislature, yet he said he did not wish the judges of Pennsylvania to exercise such a power as that employed in Holmes v. Walton, because it seemed dangerous.[36]

The next precedent we shall consider is the Virginia case of Commonwealth v. Caton,[37] where we find that Judge Wythe and

[36] Sparks, "Life of Gouverneur Morris," vol. 3, p. 438.
[37] 4 Call. 5.

Chancellor Blair, both members of the Convention of 1787, were of opinion that the courts had power to declare unconstitutional acts of the legislature which infringed the organic law. The dictum of Wythe indicates that the doctrine favoring such power had by this time (1782) gathered to its side some strong protagonists. He said that "if the whole legislature,—an event to be deprecated,—should attempt to overleap the bounds prescribed to them by the people, I, in administering the public justice of the country, will meet the united powers at my seat in this tribunal, and, pointing to the Constitution, will say to them, here is the limit of your authority, and hither shall you go, but no further."

Another case worthy of attention is Trevett v. Weeden,[38] decided in 1786. The controversy arose out of a state statute passed to aid paper currency. It provided

---

[38] Thayer, "Cases on Constitutional Law," p. 73. For an interesting discussion of this case, see article by Charles Warren in Yale Law Journal, November, 1922.

for the summary conviction of any one declining to receive such money. James M. Varnum, later a member of Congress, as counsel for defendant, pleaded that the act was void, because it denied trial by jury, and therefore infringed the charter of Rhode Island, which had been tacitly adopted as the state Constitution. He maintained that the legislators derived their power from the Constitution, and hence could not change it without destroying the very foundation of their authority.[39] He further asserted the right of the judiciary to interpret the Constitution, saying in part: "The true distinction lies in this: That the legislative have the uncontrollable power of making laws not repugnant to the Constitution; the judiciary have the sole power of judging of those laws, and are bound to execute them, but cannot admit any act of the legislature as law, which is against the Constitution." His logic appealed to the judges, who declared the statute in question to be uncon-

[39] Coxe, "Judicial Power." p. 240.

stitutional. The General Assembly of Rhode Island, resenting what they deemed an arbitrary usurpation of judicial authority, summoned the members of the court to appear and explain. The judges showed the courage of their convictions, and, upon answering the summons, earnestly reiterated the reasons for their decision, protesting against dismissal from office. Although they were not impeached, the Assembly took care, at the expiration of their terms, that only the Chief Justice should be reappointed. The decision, however, met with widespread approval, and Varnum used the opportunity thus afforded to popularize himself and the case by means of a contemporary pamphlet.[40]

With the memory of Trevett v. Weeden fresh in their minds, the delegates assembled in Philadelphia for the Constitutional Convention of 1787, but, before

[40] For details and incidents of the case, see Thayer, "Cases on Constitutional Law," p. 75; McMaster, "History of the United States," Vol. I, p. 338; Warren, "Earliest Cases of Judicial Review," Yale Law Journal, November, 1922, pp. 18–22.

any conclusion as to the power of the courts over legislation had been reached, another state joined the ranks of those asserting the right of judicial review. In May, 1787, the Court of Conference of North Carolina, in Bayard v. Singleton,[41] decided that an act of the state legislature, abolishing the common-law right of trial by jury in certain instances, was unconstitutional. James Iredell, one of the first justices of the United States Supreme Court, was chief counsel for the plaintiff, and had associated with him William R. Davie, who was attending the Constitutional Convention when the decision was rendered; even prior to Iredell's retainer as counsel, and before the case had reached the appellate court, he had taken an active interest in the contest which centered around it. In August, 1786, signing himself "An Elector," Iredell addressed a letter "To the Public," [42] in which he forcefully

---

[41] 1 Martin (N. C.) 48.

[42] The letter is printed in full in Coxe's "Judicial Power," pp. 253–258.

presented the arguments favoring the doctrine we are discussing. "The power of the Assembly," he said, "is limited and defined by the Constitution. It is a creature of the Constitution. * * * The people have chosen to be governed under such and such principles. They have not chosen to be governed, or promised to submit upon any other; and the Assembly have no more right to obedience on other terms than any different power on earth has a right to govern us; for we have as much agreed to be governed by the Turkish Divan as by our own General Assembly otherwise than on the express terms prescribed. * * * The great argument is that, though the Assembly have not a *right* to violate the Constitution, yet if they *in fact* do so, the only remedy is, either by a humble petition that the law may be repealed, or a universal resistance of the people; but that in the meantime, their act, whatever it is, is to be obeyed as law, for the judicial power is not to presume to question the power of an act of Assembly."

After refuting contentions favoring the two remedies suggested, Iredell continued: "It remains to be inquired whether the judicial power hath any authority to interfere in such a case. The duty of that power, I conceive, in all cases, is to decide according to the laws of the state. It will not be denied, I suppose, that the constitution is a law of the state as well as an act of assembly, with this difference only, that it is the fundamental law, and unalterable by the legislature, which derives all its power from it. * * * For that reason, an act of assembly, inconsistent with the constitution, is void, and cannot be obeyed, without disobeying the superior law to which we are previously and irrevocably bound. The judges, therefore, must take care, at their peril, that every act of assembly they presume to enforce is warranted by the constitution, since, if it is not, they act without lawful authority." The views of Iredell were echoed in the opinion of the North Carolina court, which evoked widespread discussion.

In addition to the state precedents already mentioned, there was another class of cases, during the critical period leading up to the Convention, that deserves passing notice. I refer to the various decisions, of which the New York case of Rutgers v. Waddington [43] is the most conspicuous, where the state courts declared void acts of their legislatures because conflicting with the Treaty of Peace negotiated by the central government. In fact, on the signing of the treaty, the Congress of the Confederation asked the states to revise their laws, so as to make them conform to the terms agreed upon with England, and, on March 21, 1787, it unanimously recommended that the several states should adopt identical statutes, authorizing and requiring their courts to nullify laws found by them to be incompatible with the terms of the treaty. In a circular letter advising the states of this action, Congress suggested that, "by repealing in general terms all

---

[43] The case is discussed in detail in Coxe's "Judicial Power," pp. 223–233.

acts and clauses repugnant to the treaty, the *business will be turned over to its proper department, viz., the judicial, and the courts of law will find no difficulty in deciding whether any particular act or clause is or is not contrary to the treaty."* [44] Perhaps these last named cases are not precedents, in a strictly legal sense, for judicial review, because the authority involved was exercised by the courts at the behest of the legislature, and, also, because the acts nullified were found to conflict with a treaty made by a superior government. Nevertheless they must be recognized as instances, —many of which were watched with general concern,—where state courts declared acts of their legislatures void; and this fact most likely left its impressions on the popular mind as consistent with the system of judicial review to which it had become, or was then becoming, accustomed.

---

[44] Journals of Congress (1823 Ed.) vol. 4, pp. 735–738.

## VI. THE CONSTITUTIONAL CONVENTION OF 1787

The delegates to the Constitutional Convention of 1787 must have been influenced largely by the incidents and precedents already discussed. It is impossible to determine just how many of these uncommon men were ready to favor any particular idea, and, for present purposes. this is unnecessary. What is important, and what we do know, is that from various sources there were brought to the Convention sentiments and beliefs which, as they were discussed and developed, became a body of principles, some of them being written down as the letter of the Constitution, and others necessarily implied as essential to a carrying out of the provisions expressed.

One of the questions, which from time to time presented itself to the Convention, concerned the best method of protecting against legislative encroachment the rights, powers, and restrictions embodied in the Constitution; for, if that instrument was to be paramount, and remain so, it was apparent there must be some practical means of peaceably preserving its supremacy from infringements by jealous or heedless lawmakers. The spectacle of the disregarded Treaty of Paris was ever before the delegates showing the need of a practical way to enforce the mandates of the central government and to keep it from further humiliation and contempt at home and abroad. By considering the discussions in the Convention, on the several methods designed and proposed to provide against infringements of the Constitution, we can at least ascertain the opinions and probable intent of the framers on the question of the right of judicial review, and we shall see the power was even then generally recognized.

Shortly after the Convention met (May 29, 1787), Randolph brought forth and, with his colleagues, advocated the so-called "Virginia Plan," providing for a strong central government administered through three arms, of which the legislative should be bicameral. To safeguard the delegated powers, the following checks and balances were embodied in the scheme: (1) Congress should have the right to veto state laws, which, in its opinion might contravene the Articles of Union,[45] and (2) a Council of Revision, consisting of the executive and a convenient number of the national judiciary, was to be created and empowered to examine and approve all acts of Congress before they should become operative.[46] The first of these two suggestions, though subsequently disapproved, was recommended by the Committee of the Whole in its report of June 13th;[47] whereas, the second met with persistent opposition, for reasons pertinent to our present inquiry. It is the refusal to incorporate into the Constitution

---

[45] The Sixth Resolution,—Farrand, "Records of the Federal Convention," vol. 1, p. 21.

[46] The Eighth Resolution,—Farrand, "Records," etc., vol. 1, p. 21.

[47] Farrand, "Records," p. 236.

this Council of Revision idea which most
of the opponents of our present system
point to as conclusive evidence that the
framers did not intend the courts to exercise the right of judicial review,—although
the debates and subsequent proceedings
of the Convention indicate quite the contrary, as I shall show.

On June 4th, five days after its submis-
sion, the proposal to create a Council of
Revision was tabled on motion of Gerry,
of Massachusetts,[48] who said in the course
of the debate that the judges could sufficiently protect the judicial department
against encroachment by their exposition
of the laws, which involved a power of deciding on the constitutionality of legislative enactments; in some states, he added,
"the judges had actually set aside laws as
being against the Constitution, and this
was done, too, with general approbation."
King, also of Massachusetts, who seconded the motion to table, observed that the
judges "ought to be able to expound the

---

[48] Id. p. 104.

law as it should come before them free from the bias of having participated in its formation." [49]

As time went on, the dissatisfaction of the smaller states with the developments in the Convention became increasingly apparent, and finally, at a series of evening meetings, the delegates from these states drew up a plan calculated to protect their interests. This "New Jersey Plan," [50] as it is usually called, was doomed to defeat, but one of its features,[51] making acts of Congress and treaties the "supreme law of the respective states," by which the state judges should "be bound in their decisions," survived, and was subsequently adopted in a broader form. In view of the fact that at least seven of the nine men who framed the New Jersey Plan are known to have favored judicial review,[52] there seems little doubt about the "supreme law" proviso it contained being

[49] Id. pp. 97, 98.
[50] Id. pp. 242–245.
[51] The Sixth Resolution, Id. p. 245.
[52] Meigs, "The Judiciary and the Constitution," p. 136.

intended as an adoption of that method of control, at least so far as state legislation was concerned. That part of the plan, however, was not referred to in the debate of the Committee of the Whole, and on June 19th the New Jersey scheme was rejected and the amended Virginia Plan reported to the Convention.[53]

The delegates spent the ensuing month battling over other, seemingly more important, problems, as to which there was vital disagreement. At this time "the fate of America was suspended by a hair."[54] It was not until the great compromise of the Constitution was effected, giving the small states equal representation in the Senate, that the Convention again turned its attention to the subject of legislation and its control.

On July 17th, the question of a congressional veto on state laws was reconsidered and subjected to sharp criticism, as being an allotment to the legislature of a judi-

[53] Farrand, "Records," vol. 1, p. 322.
[54] Farrand, "The Framing of the Constitution," p. 94.

cial function. Gouverneur Morris expressed himself as "more and more opposed to
the negative [power]," and continued,
"The proposal of it would disgust all the
states," adding, "A law that ought to be
negatived will be set aside in the judiciary
department." [55] Later the same day, Luther
Martin proposed what was substantially
the supreme law proviso of the before-
mentioned New Jersey Plan, "in substitution" [56] for the congressional veto; and his
motion was unanimously adopted. [57] Thus
the judiciary were effectively relied on to
protect the national government against
encroachments by the state legislatures.
This action is of importance, for it involved recognition of the principle of judicial review; and the fact that it created a
check on state laws only is no indication
that the national judiciary were not looked
to for enforcement of the Constitution

---

[55] Farrand, "Records of the Federal Convention," vol.
2, p. 28.

[56] Id. vol. 3, p. 286; Martin's whole letter is reproduced, pp. 286–295.

[57] Id. vol. 2, pp. 28, 29.

against Congressional encroachments. Any doubt on this score, however, is cleared by the subsequent actions of the framers, showing their intention that the judiciary should act to that end.

The very day following the adoption of Martin's plan, the Convention unanimously approved a clause, introduced by Madison, stating "that the jurisdiction of the national judiciary shall extend to cases arising under laws passed by the general legislature, and to such other questions as involved the national peace and harmony,"—a broad grant of power.[58]

A few days later the Convention voted down a second attempt to associate the executive and the supreme national judiciary as a Council of Revision to operate as a check on the federal legislature. James Wilson, on moving to establish the Council, answered the objection "that the judges, as expositors of the laws, would have an opportunity of defending their constitutional rights," by saying "there was

[58] Id. vol. 2, pp. 39, 46.

weight in this observation, but this power of the judges did not go far enough." While apparently treating the right of judicial review as conceded, he explained that "laws may be unjust, may be unwise, may be dangerous, may be destructive, and yet not be so unconstitutional as to justify the judges in refusing to give them effect."[59] Luther Martin, who then ranked as a leader of the Maryland bar, said: "As to the constitutionality of laws, that point will come before the judges in their official character; in this character they have a negative on the laws. Join them with the executive in the revision, and they will have a double negative."

Like views were expressed by Mr. Mason, of Virginia, and others, on both sides of the question before the house.[60] Madison seconded Wilson's motion and approved of the council, not as a substitute for judicial review, but as an "additional check" against legislative encroachment,

---

[59] Id. vol. 2, p. 73.
[60] Speech of Douglas A. Brown, p. 19 of this lecture.

and another bulwark to the Constitution.[61]
The motion was defeated after a lengthy
debate, in which the right of the courts to
set aside legislative acts in the course of
judicial proceedings was repeatedly asserted.[62]  Madison, undaunted by his failure,
on August 15th once more advanced his
pet scheme, in a disguised form.  This met
with no better success.  Pinckney's argument that the creation of any such council would serve to embroil the judges in
legislative affairs, thus giving "a previous
tincture to their opinions," [63] and Gerry's
reminder that the proposition had been
previously rejected and the question settled, served to satisfy the convention that
their former decision should stand.  It is
significant that both those favoring and
those opposing the national revisory council seem to have recognized and approved
of the federal judges exercising the power
of judicial review over national legislation.

---

[61] Farrand, "Records," etc., vol. 2, p. 74.
[62] Id. pp. 72–80.
[63] Id. p. 298.

The difference of opinion related, not to the existence of a right of review, it went rather to the sufficiency of that power as a legislative check.

On August 23d, the Convention voted to amend Martin's supreme law clause, making it acknowledge *the Constitution,* as well as the laws and treaties made in pursuance thereof, to be "the supreme law of the several states," which should bind the state judges in their decisions.[64] Another important alteration of this clause was made in Committee, on September 12th, when the words "supreme law of the several states" were changed to read "supreme law of the land,"—a significant substitution in view of the fact that four of the five members of the Committee are on record as favoring judicial review of legislation.[65] The action of the Committee was approved by the Convention on September 14th, thus writing these provisions in

---

[64] Id. p. 389.

[65] Id. p. 603. On the views of the Committee, see Beard, "The Supreme Court and the Constitution," p. 65.

the form in which they now appear in Article VI of the Constitution.

Finally, on August 27th, the Convention expressly extended the federal judicial power "to all cases arising under this Constitution," [66] thus, to my mind, settling the right of the federal courts to review acts of Congress alleged to be violative of the Constitution.

The insertion in the Constitution of these provisions, that it should be the supreme law of the land, binding all state judges (article VI), and the grant of appellate jurisdiction to the federal Supreme Court (article III, section 2), are generally considered as vesting in that tribunal power to review state legislation; that this power is more pronouncedly shown in the Constitution than the power to review acts of Congress may be explained by the fact that every one realized the popular feeling of opposition to any outside control of state agencies, as representing a strong prejudice which had to

---

[66] Farrand, "Records," etc., vol. 2, p. 430.

be reckoned with and plainly provided against, whereas a possible future jealousy between the judicial and legislative departments of the national government called for no such consideration or treatment. Again, the history of the Convention, the debates therein, and the failure, after efforts, to agree on any other formula for the protection of the Constitution against possible congressional encroachments, strongly suggests that the delegates must have tacitly concluded it was best to frame an instrument whose every line was consistent with the doctrine of judicial review, to trust to that known plan, and await its further development so far as national legislation was concerned, rather than to embarrass that development by an attempted definition,—which open method is a course often pursued by wise men.

So far as the evidence shows, the delegates refused to sanction a congressional veto upon state legislation, because of the friction which such a plan would entail, and rejected the Council of Revision because it would duplicate the existing power of the courts to declare unconstitutional acts void. By a slow process of evolution, of which I have mentioned merely the salient steps, it made the Constitution the "supreme law of the land," binding upon the state courts, and gave to the federal judiciary power over all cases arising under it. It must be remembered that article III, section 1, of the Constitution expressly vests the judicial power of the United States in the Supreme Court and such inferior courts as Congress may, from time to time, establish; and section 2 provides that the judicial power shall extend to all cases, in law and equity, arising under the Constitution, the laws of the United States, and treaties made by their authority. The net result is to bestow upon, or recognize as belonging to, the national courts, within the field of their jurisdiction, the usual judicial functions, including, of course, the power of interpreting the laws of the United States and hence, necessarily the Constitution, which expressly declares itself the supreme law of the land. This right to interpret the Constitution, when brought before them in pending litigation, incidentally gave to the federal courts the right to safeguard the latter against legislative aggression or mistakes of such a nature as to infringe the organic law. It was unnecessary to express this power in plainer language, because, as previously stated, its sponsors regarded it inherent in the courts, composed as they are of expositors of the law, fundamental and otherwise. "The interpretation of the laws," said Hamilton, in the Federalist "is the proper and peculiar power of the courts. A constitution is in fact and must be regarded by the judges as a fundamental law. It therefore belongs to them to ascertain its meaning, as well as the meaning of any particular act proceeding from the legislative body. If there should happen to be an irreconcilable variance between the two, that which has the superior obligation and validity ought, of course, to be prefer-

red." [67]   This view, so well expressed by
Hamilton, seems to represent the matured
opinion of the majority of the Convention
of 1787; and, to reiterate, they evidently
regarded the doctrine as so interwoven in
the whole scheme of government as to
need no more exact grant in the Constitution than that contained in the before-
quoted provisions.

## VII.   OPINIONS OF THE FRAMERS

By this time, as we have seen, quite a
number of the framers had placed themselves squarely on record as advocates of
the system of judicial review, while only a
few seem to have opposed it openly.   Of
those who kept silent it seems safe to assert that many approved of the doctrine
while others were probably in much the
same predicament as Dickinson, who expressed dislike for the system it involved,

---

[67] The Federalist, No. 78, reproduced in Thayer, "Cases
on Constitutional Law," p. 89.

but confessed his inability to suggest a practical substitute.[68]

Where the existence of a power, long
exercised, can be reconciled with the language of the Constitution and also appears
to be embodied in it, the contemporaneous
opinions of the framers form cogent evidence to meet a contention such as we now
have to combat,—that the system of judicial review was never intended as part of
our form of government; therefore it is
pertinent, for present purposes, to heed
such opinions, and these have been col-
lected by numerous writers, who, I am
bound to admit, differ in their conclusions.

The most thorough search on this subject has been made by Professor Beard,
of Columbia University,[69] who lists twenty-five of the fifty-five members of the
Convention as those whose character, abil-
ity, influence, and interest made them the
dominant element. Of these twenty-five,

---

[68] Farrand, "Records," vol. 2, p. 299.

[69] Charles A. Beard, "The Supreme Court and the
Constitution."

Professor Beard concludes that seventeen declared directly or indirectly for the right of judicial review; he finds five delegates, at the most, who were probably opposed to the doctrine, and but one of these appears in the influential group.[70] The only article I have read, which, with any seriousness, attacks these conclusions was written by Mr. Horace A. Davis;[71] and it has been rather well disposed of by Mr. Frank E. Melvin,[72] who, going even further than Professor Beard, presents evidence to prove that "of the fifty-five actual members of the federal Convention, some thirty-two to forty of them, that is, two-thirds of the Convention, including nearly every influential member, upheld, or accepted, the right of the courts to disregard as law an unconstitutional legislative act, while [only] four or five apparently op-

---

[70] Id. pp. 17, 54.

[71] "Annulment of Legislation by the Supreme Court," 7 Am. Pol. Science Rev. 541.

[72] "The Judicial Bulwark of the Constitution," 8 Am. Pol. Science Rev. pp. 167, 195–201.

posed it." The views of some ten members remain substantially unascertained.[73]

## VIII. THE DOCTRINE IN THE RATIFYING CONVENTIONS

No less pertinent, as confirmatory evidence, are the utterances of some of the leaders in the ratifying conventions of the several states; it was these bodies which gave the ultimate stamp of approval to the Constitution. They were concerned chiefly with federal judicial control over state statutes, a somewhat different matter from judicial review of congressional enactments; nevertheless, the latter subject was brought up in several of the state conventions, of which I shall mention only the most striking instances.

The first convention was held in Pennsylvania, where James Wilson, an acknowledged champion of judicial review,

[73] Melvin, "The Judicial Bulwark of the Constitution," supra, p. 191.

speaking on the judicial power clause, said: "If a law should be made inconsistent with those powers vested by this instrument in Congress, the judges, as a consequence of their independence, and the particular powers of government being defined, will declare such a law to be null and void, for the power of the Constitution predominates; anything, therefore, that shall be enacted by Congress contrary thereto will not have the force of law." [74]

Similar notes of enlightenment were sounded in the Maryland convention by Luther Martin,[75] and in the Connecticut convention by Oliver Ellsworth. The latter, soon to become a Supreme Court justice, stated clearly that "this Constitution defines the extent of the powers of the general government. If the general legislature should at any time overleap their limits, the judicial department is a constitutional check. If the United States go be-

---

[74] Elliot's "Debates," vol. 2, p. 489.
[75] Id. vol. 1, p. 380.

yond their powers, if they make a law which the Constitution does not authorize, it is void; and the judicial power,—the national judges, who, to secure their impartiality, are to be made independent,—will declare it to be void." [76]

During the sessions of the New York convention there appeared (May, 1788) No. 78 of The Federalist, which was unquestionably widely read by those engaged in considering the ratification of the Constitution. In this number, Hamilton discussed "The right of the courts to pronounce legislative acts void," calling it "a doctrine of great importance in *all American* constitutions." He said: "There is no position which depends on clearer principles than that every act of a delegated authority, contrary to the tenor of the commission under which it is exercised, is void. No legislative act, therefore, contrary to the Constitution, can be valid,"—adding, "To deny this would be to affirm that the

[76] Id. vol. 2, p. 196. Cf. Farrand, vol. 3, p. 240.

deputy is greater than his principal; that the servant is above his master; that the representatives of the people are superior to the people themselves." He then went on to say that the interpretation of the laws is the proper and peculiar province of the courts which must declare void all enactments repugnant to the fundamental law.[77]

The most significant of all utterances in the ratifying conventions is found in Virginia, where Patrick Henry opposed the right of judicial review with characteristic force. He attacked the whole judiciary article long and bitterly, ending with the words: "Old as I am, it is probable I may yet have the appellation of rebel. * * * As this government [Constitution] stands, I despise and abhor it."[78] Patrick Henry was answered by John Marshall, who had been chosen by the Constitutionalist leaders of Virginia for the critical task of de-

[77] Thayer, "Cases on Constitutional Law," pp. 89, 90.
[78] Elliot, "Debates," vol. 3, pp. 539–546.

fending the judiciary article. In the course of his defense, Marshall stated the doctrine which, fifteen years later, he was to announce from the Supreme Bench in Marbury v. Madison. "Has the government of the United States power to make laws on every subject?" queried the future Chief Justice. "Can they make laws affecting the mode of transferring property, or contracts, or claims between citizens of the same state? Can they go beyond the delegated powers? If," he asserted, "they [Congress] were to make a law not warranted by any of the powers enumerated, it would be considered by the judges as an infringement of the Constitution which they are to guard. They would not consider such a law as coming under their jurisdiction; they would declare it void." Then Marshall spoke these true and significant words: "To what quarter will you look for protection from an infringement of the Constitution, if you will not give the power to the judiciary? There is no other body that can afford such a protection." [79]

How, in the face of all this evidence, can it justly be claimed that our present system of judicial review was not intended by those who framed and adopted the federal Constitution?

---

[79] Id. p. 553.

# SECOND LECTURE

## IX. GROWTH OF THE DOCTRINE UNDER THE CONSTITUTION
### 1789–1803

In my last lecture I considered the growth of the doctrine of judicial review down to the beginning of our national life under the Constitution. Scarcely had the Federalists assumed the reins of government, and begun to direct the destinies of the country, than there appeared a recognition by the national Legislature itself of the right of the Supreme Court to declare void such acts of Congress as breached the Constitution. Section 25 of the Judiciary Act of 1789 provided that the federal Supreme Court might examine, and reverse or affirm, any decision of a state court holding an act of Congress unconstitutional.[80] If the highest tribunal

---

[80] See G. T. Curtis, "Life of Buchanan," vol. 1, p. 112 et seq., for interesting discussion of section 25 of the Act of 1789.

could, by affirming the judgment of a state court, declare void a statute of the national legislature, the conclusion seems inescapable that it was intended the same tribunal might exercise a like power when acting directly; there is no substantial ground on which to base a distinction. "Indeed," Professor Beard very pertinently remarks, "it would seem absurd to assume that an act of Congress might be annulled by a state court with the approval of the Supreme Court, but not by the Supreme Court directly." [81] Furthermore the credit for the drafting and passing of this bill is due in large measure to Oliver Ellsworth, a staunch supporter of the doctrine of judicial review.

The first assertion of the right by the federal courts occurred in Pennsylvania. In 1792, the national legislature passed an act directing the circuit courts to hear petitions of applicants for pensions, their findings to be subject to review by the

[81] Beard, "The Supreme Court and the Constitution," p. 45.

secretary of war and by Congress. When this statute came before James Wilson and his associates on the Pennsylvania circuit, the court refused to proceed upon the petition presented. The "reasons for [their] conduct," and its importance, are shown by a letter which the judges addressed to the President protesting that the Pension Act directed them to issue decrees upon matters of a nonjudicial nature, and subjected their findings to legislative and executive revision. "Such * * * control," they said, "we deemed radically inconsistent with the independence of that judicial power which is vested in the courts"; and they went on to state their unpleasant feelings at finding it necessary to act contrary to the express directions of Congress.[82] This, "The First Hayburn Case," as it is called for purposes of distinction, is generally conceded to be the initial decision of the federal courts hold-

[82] "Note to Hayburn's Case," 2 Dall. 410–414, 1 L. Ed. 436; Prof. Max Farrand, "The First Hayburn Case," 12 Amer. Hist. Rev., pp. 281–285.

ing unconstitutional an act of the national legislature.[83]  A few men, both in and out of Congress, ventured to raise the cry of "impeachment," but they were quickly silenced,[84] for everywhere the conception of the courts as guardians of the Constitution seemed to be gaining ground.

In 1795, Justice Paterson, of the United States Supreme Court, while charging a jury on circuit, stated the underlying principle in terms which were bound to make a vivid and lasting impression. He said: "The Constitution is the work or will of the people themselves, in their  *  *  * sovereign capacity; law is the work or will of the legislature in their derivative and subordinate capacity. The one is the work of the creator; the other of the creature. The Constitution fixes limits to the exercise of legislative authority, and prescribes the orbit within which it must

---

[83] Meigs, "The Judiciary and the Constitution," p. 184; Haines, "American Doctrine of Judicial Supremacy," p. 158.

[84] Corwin, "Doctrine of Judicial Review," p. 50 and note.

move. In short, gentlemen, the Constitution is the sun of the political system, around which all legislative, executive, and judicial bodies must revolve. Whatever may be the case in other countries, yet in this there can be no doubt that every act of the legislature, repugnant to the Constitution, is absolutely void." [85]

The year following, the Supreme Court in banc had occasion to consider its power of review, when, in Hylton v. United States, [86] an act of Congress taxing carriages was attacked as unconstitutional. Inasmuch as the statute was held to be a valid exercise of the taxing power, Justice Chase did not think it necessary to decide, at the time, whether the court possessed the power, under the Constitution, to declare an act of Congress void. He did say, however, that if such power existed he would exercise it only in very clear cases; and this is still the rule with all courts.

---

[85] Van Horne v. Dorrance, 2 Dall. 304, 308, 1 L. Ed. 391.

[86] 3 Dall. 171, 175, 1 L. Ed. 556 (1796).

Justice Chase displayed a like hesitancy in Calder v. Bull,[87] decided in 1798, where the validity of a state statute was involved. Iredell, in the same litigation, entertained no doubts on the power of the courts to declare legislation unconstitutional; he thus expressed the guiding principle for the exercise of this power: "As the authority * * * is of a delicate and awful nature, the court will never resort to [it] but in a clear and urgent case."

Several years later, in Cooper v. Telfair,[88] Justice Chase summed up the current attitude of his bench by stating it was the general opinion frequently expressed by all the bar, and even by some of the judges upon circuit, that the Supreme Court could declare void an act of Congress which plainly conflicts with the Constitution; yet he added that, in the absence of a formal adjudication of the point by the tribunal itself, it must remain an open question.

Thus, on the eve of the unexpected ap-

---

[87] 3 Dall. 386, 392, 1 L. Ed. 648.
[88] 4 Dall. 14, 19, 1 L. Ed. 721 (1800).

pointment of John Marshall as Chief Justice, the Supreme Court was slowly, perhaps timidly, approaching the principle of Marbury v. Madison. Before considering that monumental decision it may be helpful to observe what had been happening to judicial review in the states.

We have already noted that, at the time of the Convention of 1787, there were three actual decisions, by as many state courts (New Jersey, Connecticut, and Rhode Island), holding acts void because in conflict with state Constitutions. Between the calling of the Convention and 1803, when Marbury v. Madison was decided, seven more state courts (North Carolina, New Hampshire, South Carolina, Virginia, Pennsylvania, Kentucky, and Maryland) joined the ranks of those asserting and defending the right of judicial review.[89]

---

[89] See note on the subject in Corwin's "Doctrine of Judicial Review," pp. 75–78; and see Meigs, "The Judiciary and the Constitution," p. 177. Compare article by B. F. Moore, Columbia Historical Studies, vol. 54, pp. 11, 31; and Table of State Cases, Haines, "American Doctrine of Judicial Supremacy," pp. 74–77.

Thus by 1803, nine of the thirteen original states and one of those newly admitted (Kentucky) had taken a stand in favor of the doctrine which Marshall was about to assert on behalf of the Supreme Court.

## X. MARBURY v. MADISON

In order to understand properly the doctrine of judicial review from its national aspect, we must consider the case of Marbury v. Madison in the light of those historic events which immediately preceded it. During the closing years of the eighteenth century, the great Federalist party, which had laid so firmly the foundations of American political institutions, was fast declining. Thomas Jefferson was leaving no stone unturned to quicken its downfall and to make his States' Rights theory a reality. The publication of dispatches from John Marshall and the other envoys sent to France on the X. Y. Z. Mission revealed conduct on the part of the French government which even Washington characterized as "outrageous." [90] It affected Adams and the other Federalist leaders to such an extent that, in the summer of 1798, they passed the drastic Alien and Sedition Laws. Immediately there began to rise a wave of opposition, which later swept the Federalists from office and attained for Jefferson the goal of his ambition.

This resentment first found notable expression in the Virginia and Kentucky Resolutions of 1798, declaring the Alien and Sedition Laws void, and calling on the states to assert their rights against the imperious national government. Most of the state legislatures, however, were still in the hands of Federalist majorities,[91] who refused to countenance any such revolutionary measures. They pointed to the national judges as the proper functionaries to determine the constitutionality of acts of Congress; so, in a sense, these replies were victories for judicial review, but the Alien and Sedition Laws remained ex-

[90] Beveridge, "Life of Marshall," vol. 2, p. 341.
[91] Id. vol. 3, p. 105.

tant, and their rigid enforcement did much to bring the Federalist judges into disfavor, thus attracting a host of recruits to the Republican colors. Jefferson and his party triumphed at the ensuing election of 1800, and the party of Washington went down to defeat.

In despair lest the States' Rights doctrine should encompass all departments and destroy the Union, the Federalists, to use the words of Jefferson, "retreated into the judiciary." They spent their last months in power formulating and passing the Judiciary Act of 1801, an admirable law, correcting numerous defects in the Act of 1789. One provision abolished the circuit duties of the Supreme Court justices, and provided for circuit judges,— a provision worthy in itself, but containing a joker which enabled Adams, with the aid of the Senate, to fill the newly created positions before his term expired. He appointed strong Federalists, whom the Republicans contemptuously called "midnight judges," because, they said, the appointees were rushed into office as late as midnight on March 3, 1801.

No sooner had Jefferson assumed control than his followers launched an attack against the Judiciary Act of 1801, with the purpose of repealing it. The debates in Congress, begun on January 6, 1802, were long and acrimonious. The Federalists took the position that the proposed act, abolishing the recently created circuit judgeships, would materially weaken the national judiciary; that the Constitution would permit no such destruction of one department of the government by another; and that Marshall and his associates would declare the statute void, if passed. The Republicans denied the right of the Supreme Court to annul acts of Congress, asserting that the power of each department was exclusive within its sphere of action, and that the legislature had the final say as to the constitutionality of its own enactments. If Marshall and the Federalist judges should dare to attempt an annulment of the Repeal Act, then, the Republicans declared, resort must be had to impeachment. As against this menace of impeachment, the Federalists threatened armed resistance; Bayard, their leader in the House, warned his opponents that there were many willing to spill their blood to defend the Constitution, and that, if the independence of the national judiciary were destroyed, "the moment is not far when this country is to be desolated by civil war."[92]  In the course of the debate, every existing decision and dictum which asserted the right of the courts to find legislative acts unconstitutional was cited; every argument in favor of judicial review was stated and restated; practically every reason appeared that John Marshall was to advance to sustain his conclusion in Marbury v. Madison, just one year later; indeed, Senator Beveridge, in his biography of Marshall, expresses the view that it was this debate, and the results of it, which influenced the Chief Justice to write the opinion as he did.[93]

---

[92] Id. vol. 3, p. 82.　　　　[93] Id. vol. 3, p. 75.

The Judiciary Act of 1801 was repealed, and, by February, 1803, impeachment proceedings had been started against several of the federal district judges; the intent of the Republicans to subjugate the national judiciary no longer remained a matter of doubt. Some speedy and effective action had to be taken, if the inviolability of the Constitution and the independence of our courts were to remain. John Marshall found the opportunity in the case of Marbury v. Madison,[94] then pending before the Supreme Court.

Briefly stated, the case involved the following facts: Several justices of the peace appointed by President Adams at the close of his administration had not received their commissions, though signed and sealed. They petitioned the Supreme Court for a writ of mandamus to compel Madison, who had become Secretary of State under Jefferson, to deliver these documents, and the court ruled the Secretary to show cause why

---

[94] 1 Cranch, 137, 2 L. Ed. 60.

the writ should not issue. The rule was ignored.

It was the popular belief that Madison would be ordered to deliver the commissions, that he would refuse, and a test of strength between the executive and judicial departments of the government would result; but the court pursued a far better course. Marshall thought section 13 of the Judiciary Act of 1789, which authorized the Supreme Court to issue writs of mandamus, invalid, and convinced his associates of the propriety of so holding. In view of the circumstance that his tribunal had previously sanctioned its jurisdiction to issue writs of mandamus in a proper case,[95] the boldness of selecting this occasion for formally announcing the power of review over legislation, as vested in the courts, was notable, although, as already shown, the doctrine was older than the nation itself.

Marshall's opinion is an able reiteration of those sound principles which Wilson,

---

[95] Beveridge, "Life of Marshall," vol. 3, p. 129.

Iredell, Paterson, Hamilton, and all the other exponents of judicial review had previously asserted, from the bench, in the conventions, and elsewhere. He began by deciding that Marbury, having been properly appointed to office, had a right to his commission, which was enforceable by mandamus against the Secretary of State. Section 13 of the Act of 1789 purported to give the Supreme Court power to issue writs of mandamus, he held, and the mandate would have to go out if the provision in question was constitutional. He then proceeded to consider the validity of the section, concluding that, when article III of the Constitution conferred on the Supreme Court original jurisdiction in certain specified cases, it impliedly excluded all others, and thus, in effect, denied to Congress the power to expand the jurisdiction originally granted. Having arrived at this conclusion, Marshall turned to consider "the question whether an act repugnant to the Constitution can become the law of the land." "This is a question," said the Chief Justice, "deeply interesting to the United States, but happily not of an intricacy proportioned to its interest. It seems only necessary to recognize certain principles, supposed to have been long and well established, to decide it. That the people have an original right to establish, for their future government such principles as, in their opinion, shall most conduce to their own happiness is the basis on which the whole American fabric has been erected. * * * This original and supreme will organizes the government, and assigns to different departments their respective powers. It may either stop here, or establish certain limits not to be transcended by those departments. The government of the United States is of the latter description. The powers of the legislature are defined and limited, and, that those limits may not be mistaken or forgotten, the Constitution is written. To what purpose are powers limited, and to what purpose is that limitation committed to writing, if these limits may, at any time,

be passed by those intended to be restrain-
ed. * * * It is a proposition too plain
to be contested that the Constitution con-
trols any legislative act repugnant to it,
or that the legislature may alter the Constitution by an ordinary act. Between
these alternatives there is no middle
ground. The Constitution is either a superior paramount law, unchangeable by ordinary means, or it is on a level with ordinary legislative acts, and, like other acts, is
alterable when the legislature shall please
to alter it. If the former part of the alter-
native be true, then a legislative act contrary to the Constitution is not law; if
the latter part be true, then written constitutions are absurd attempts, on the part
of the people, to limit a power in its own
nature illimitable. Certainly all those who
have framed written constitutions contemplate them as forming the fundamental
and paramount law of the nation, and, consequently, the theory of every such government must be that an act of the legislature, repugnant to the Constitution, is

void. This theory is essentially attached to a written constitution and is consequently to be considered, by this court, as one of the fundamental principles of our society. * * * It is emphatically the province and duty of the judicial department to say what the law is. * * * If two laws conflict with each other, the courts must decide on the operation of each." [96]

Thus did the great Chief Justice skillfully state the logical arguments in favor of the right of judicial review,—which, as we have seen, had been previously threshed out by many other leaders of thought. That this official pronouncement of a judicial guardianship of the Constitution was in no sense startling is evidenced by the fact that, at the time it went forth, little popular attention was paid to Marshall's opinion. It served, however, as a spur to the courts in exerting their right of control over unconstitutional legislation, and, gradually, the rising generations came to

[96] 1 Cranch, 176, 177, 2 L. Ed. 60.

consider the judiciary as the natural pre-
server of our constitutional liberties.

Those who regard Marbury v. Madison
as containing false doctrine and representing usurpation of authority point to Marshall's failure to cite the precedents we
have noted as evidence of a lack of belief
in them and an admission on his part of
their weakness. Such is far from the
case.[97] He was a member of the Virginia
ratifying convention, and, in defending the
judiciary article of the Constitution, had
said the judges would declare void an act
infringing the organic law.[98] We know
that he carefully studied the Federalist,
which was commonly looked upon as a
mirror of the views of the convention, and
I have already shown a few of the strong
arguments for judicial control set forth in
that publication. Certainly Marshall must
have read the press accounts of the congressional debate of 1802, when all the for-

---

[97] Beveridge, "Life of Marshall," vol. 3, Appendix C,
pp. 611–615.
[98] See first lecture, supra, p. 63.

mer precedents were quoted in detail, for he was in Washington at the time and the debate was of great public interest.. In fact, it is more than likely that he heard the most notable of those debates, and was fully informed as to the precedents.

If, then, Marshall was familiar with all these developments in the growth of the doctrine, why did he not refer to them in his historic opinion? This question cannot be authoritatively answered, but Mr. Dougherty, in his book on the Federal Judiciary,[99] very plausibly suggests that it was because Marshall thought the true meaning and intent of the Constitution was to be found in the language of the instrument itself. Moreover, in judicial proceedings, when courts are construing writings, they, as a rule, neither seek nor cite the views of those who framed them. Again, much of the information relating to the views of the framers, which we now enjoy, was unavailable for citation when

[99] Dougherty, "Power of Federal Judiciary Over Legislation," p. 5.

Marshall wrote Marbury v. Madison, since the records of the conventions had not then been made public, and therefore could not have been cited authentically. At the present time, however, these opinions are interesting as matters of history and helpful in showing the weakness of the contention that the power of judicial review was not contemplated by those who planned and adopted the Constitution.

## XI.  FOUNDERS INTENDED TO ADOPT THE DOCTRINE

No attempt has been made in these lectures to trace the growth of the doctrine of judicial review in all its details. I have recited merely the major events in the history of the adoption of the doctrine, and quoted only a very few statements from the array of pertinent utterances by those men who built the foundations on which our peace, prosperity and contentment rest, —so far as governmental institutions can effect such things. Nevertheless sufficient evidence has been adduced to show that the present system did not originate in any usurpation by Marshall and his associates, but finds its antecedents and psychological support in (1) the system of review of colonial legislation by the English Privy Council, which existed prior to the Revolution; [100] (2) the then prevailing dissatisfaction caused by the acts of an omnipotent Parliament; (3) the favorable impression made on the colonists by the dicta of Lord Coke, —which attacked the idea of legislative omnipotency and suggested the thought of the paramountcy of a fundamental law; and, finally, (4) the desire of our ancestors for a code of certain, fundamental, controlling rules, with a practical way to make them work. These, and other institutions, situations, doctrines, impressions, convic-

---

[100] See Roscoe Pound's pamphlet, "An Introduction to American Law," where (page 16) he states: "As a result of the English revolution of 1688, Parliament became supreme; in America, where courts had been required to pass upon the validity of colonial legislation with respect to colonial charters, the idea was familiar at the time our Constitutions were adopted, and for that and other reasons passed into our constitutional law."

tions, and desires each and all had their influence in bringing about the growth and adoption by the founders of this country of the system under which we are now operating.

It is inconceivable that, after the colonists had won their liberty through years of bloodshed, they should have written a code of fundamental laws, to guard and preserve that liberty according to the principles on which they agreed it should be exercised, and yet contemplated no method of enforcing such laws. Had they so acted, the Constitution would have been a vain thing, and not the great and paramount law which they expressly said it should be. Can it be supposed that when, in article VI, section 2, the framers said the Constitution should be the supreme *law of the land,* they used these words unwittingly? Certainly not; and then, as now, the interpretation and enforcement of the law were matters belonging to the judiciary exclusively. Furthermore, the conclusion that the present method of judicial review was intended for use from the beginning of our government is strengthened and affirmed by the fact of the enactment of Judiciary Statute of 1789, the general approval of the right to pass on the validity of legislation, which has prevailed throughout the country, and the persistent acquiescence in the system for more than a century, despite the fact that the majority of the state constitutions omit all mention of it.

## XII. OPPOSITION TO THE DOCTRINE

As we have seen, there had been at prior times some public opposition to the doctrine of judicial review, and in 1856, when the Dred Scott Case was decided, a real clamor arose against the exercise of this right. The utterances of Lincoln at that time are often mistakenly relied on today by those who, because of their personal dissatisfaction with particular decisions, are prone to question the authority of our courts to declare acts of Congress unconstitutional.

Lincoln's words show, however, that he was not of their class; for, though disagreeing with the judgment in the Dred Scott Case, instead of crying "usurpation," he distinctly recognized the right of the courts to review legislation. Lincoln said: "Judicial decisions have two uses: First, to absolutely determine the case decided; and, secondly, to indicate to the public how other similar cases will be decided when they arise. * * * We believe as much as Judge Douglas (perhaps more) in obedience to and respect for the judicial department of government. We think its decisions on constitutional questions, when fully settled, should control not only the particular cases decided, but the general policy of the country, subject to be disturbed only by amendments of the Constitution as provided in that instrument itself. More than this would be revolution, but we think the Dred Scott decision is erroneous. We know the court that made it has often overruled its own decisions, and we shall do what we can to have it overrule this. We offer no resistance to it."

In our history, every outburst against judicial review has subsided after common sense and reason have had time to replace passion and prejudice, and the chronicles show that opposition to the doctrine has not consistently been the political tenet of any group or party. Such opposition manifested itself only in sporadic attacks, by different groups, predicated upon a temporary and partisan dissatisfaction with some particular decision or decisions.[101]

Perhaps the ablest man who ever attempted to oppose the doctrine was Chief Justice Gibson, of Pennsylvania, who, admitting the federal Constitution gave the judges the right to annul *state* enactments conflicting with it, denied that it conferred power on any court to set aside acts of its co-ordinate legislative body. These views he put forth in a dissenting opinion in

---

[101] See Charles Warren's Article in Yale Law Journal, Nov., 1922, p. 28.

1825.[102] Some years later, however, when this opinion was cited in argument before him, the famous Chief Justice said he had "changed" the views there expressed "for two reasons": First, because a recently held state constitutional convention, by its silence on the subject, had sanctioned the right of the court to deal with the acts of the legislature; and, next, "from experience of the necessity of the case."

Later another distinguished Pennsylvanian, Dean William Trickett, of the Dickinson Law School, launched an attack against the power, terming it "The Great Usurpation." [103] This is an able attempt to show that the doctrine of judicial review lacks constitutional basis and has not justified itself in practice. I do not know whether the Dean, like his famous townsman, Gibson, has changed his mind, but I hope such is the case.

---

[102] Eakin v. Raub, 12 Serg. & R. 330, 339.

[103] 40 Am. Law Review, 356–376. See, also, "Judicial Dispensation from Congressional Statutes," 41 Am. Law Rev. 65; "Judicial Nullification of Acts of Congress," North Amer. Rev. vol. 185, p. 848.

Until quite lately, the voice of opposition had largely died away, and the judicial power to declare legislation unconstitutional seemed to have the almost unanimous approval of our people; but certain modern critics, granting the right of judicial review to have some possible basis, take the position that the fruits of the doctrine have not been such as to justify its continuance in practice.

This is substantially the attitude of Mr. Jackson H. Ralston, who made a study of the subject at the instance of the American Federation of Labor. In a recent article,[104] he reviews various decisions of the United States Supreme Court setting aside acts of Congress, and concludes "that, as a protection to the individual, the jurisdiction has been almost a failure; as a political institution it has been frightfully dangerous; and as a method of social review it has been destructive of human life."

This critic relies chiefly on seven cases

---

[104] "Judicial Control over Legislatures," **54 Am. Law Rev.** 1–38, 193–230.

to substantiate his sweeping indictment,
and to show what he calls "an almost un-
interrupted series of failures, an almost in-
variable course of mischief, pursued by
the [federal] Supreme Court in its inter-
ferences with congressional legislation."
Of these seven cases, one was reversed by
the court itself,[105] and one negatived by
a constitutional amendment.[106] Two others [107] were decisions against the validity
of legislation fostered by the Federation of
Labor, at whose instance Mr. Ralston's investigation was made; so we could hardly
expect him to regard them with an unbias-
ed mind. Several decisions are criticized
by him because their effect was to frustrate
unconstitutional attempts of Congress to
better industrial conditions, to protect chil-

---

[105] Hepburn v. Griswold, 8 Wall. 603, 19 L. Ed. 513,
overruled in Legal Tender Cases, 12 Wall. 457, 20 L.
Ed. 287.

[106] Pollock v. Farmers' Loan & Trust Co., 157 U. S.
429, 15 Sup. Ct. 673, 39 L. Ed. 759, and 158 U. S. 601,
15 Sup. Ct. 912, 39 L. Ed. 1108, and Sixteenth Amendment.

[107] Howard v. Ill. Central R. R. Co., 207 U. S. 463, 28
Sup. Ct. 141, 52 L. Ed. 297; Adair v. U. S., 208 U S.
161, 28 Sup. Ct. 277, 52 L. Ed. 436, 13 Ann. Cas. 764.

dren and alleviate suffering; but, when considering these cases, it must be remembered that, in most instances, such matters, directly affecting the everyday life of the people, were intentionally left to the several states, as better able to pass on them according to local conditions and desires, because, at the time the Constitution was made, our forefathers, wise as they were, could not foresee present-day industrial conditions, or the common bringing together of the people by improved means of transportation and other such agencies.

Mr. Ralston presents surprisingly little evidence to sustain his general indictment of judicial review. Moreover, he examines merely legislative acts declared void, neglecting completely the very much greater number declared valid. Judicial review contemplates both of these, and it is only when we examine all of them, whether held valid or invalid, that the doctrine appears in its true perspective, and the general reluctance of the court to depart from the opinion of the law-making body becomes manifest. He also fails to give thought to the mass of forbidden, and probably objectionable, legislation which, we can well conceive, would have been passed by a sovereign Congress, unchecked by the knowledge that trained judges, with life tenure of office, stood armed with power to guard the fundamental law against all such attacks.

Our Constitution represents the settled will of the people as a whole, and to this fundamental law the Supreme Court and every other tribunal, or governmental body, must adhere, notwithstanding any apparent social or political benefits which departures might bring about, or help to accomplish. How, then, it may be asked, are we to remove a constitutional barrier to a national desire for some needed, but forbidden, reform in our social, industrial, or political system? The answer is obvious: Through an amendment,—a course which has been followed from the beginning of our history by those desirous of accomplishing something not permitted by the Constitution,[108] and which of late has proved to be not very difficult of execution, when public sentiment is systematically aroused. Is not this method of change, with its necessity, first, for action by Congress, then by the several states, far safer and much wiser than curtailing or abolishing our system of judicial review, or encouraging the courts in effect to remake the fundamental law by what, from time to time, may seem to be expedient departures therefrom?

When moved to criticize the judiciary for adherence to settled points of view as to the meaning of the federal Constitution, we must remember that, though it was written in a fine period of political reconstruction, at that time thoughts concerning protection to the individual rights of members of society were paramount; men's minds had not then commenced to center on the necessity of making laws and interpreting legal rules for the economic

---

[108] See Chisholm v. Georgia, 2 Dall. 419, 1 L. Ed. 440, and the Eleventh Amendment.

contentment of groups of people, and thus bettering the social whole. The Constitution not having been drawn with these modern ideas in view, it will, and should, take time for that which may be good in them to affect the body of our law. Desirable results in this respect cannot be forced through the medium of alterations in our legal machinery.

## XIII. SUGGESTED CHANGES IN OUR SYSTEM; PROBABLE RESULTS

The matters discussed to this point bring us naturally to a consideration of the proposed changes in our present system referred to at the beginning of these lectures.[109] The first of these[110] might well

---

[109] Such propositions are by no means novel in American history. About 1821 there was a movement to constitute the Senate an appellate tribunal above the Supreme Court; in December, 1823, a bill was proposed requiring the concurrence of seven judges in any opinion involving the validity of state or national statutes; in the following March, a Senate bill was reported from

---

[110] See note 110 on following page.

be entitled "An amendment to permit Congress to change the fundamental law whenever that body disagrees with the Supreme Court on the meaning of the Constitution." Briefly, it is this: No federal judge, in tribunals below the highest court, shall have power to declare an act of Congress unconstitutional; and when such an act is declared unconstitutional by the Supreme Court, if again passed by Congress, it will become the law of the land, thus overruling the prior judicial finding of conflict with the organic law. In other words, Congress is to be supreme and without ultimate restraint in deciding the meaning of the Constitution, so far as legislation is concerned. The actual effect of such a rule will be to give binding force

committee requiring five out of the seven judges to invalidate a state enactment; again, in 1866, another bill appeared, requiring the full court to concur in judgments invalidating legislation; and in 1867 there was a suggestion calling for concurrence of two-thirds of the judges. See Warren, "The Supreme Court in United States History," vol. II, 117, 121–124, and volume III, 171.

110 Proposed La Follette Amendment; see note 3, supra.

to legislation, even though the objects sought to be obtained are forbidden by the Constitution; for there will be no power that may say the final action of the legislature is not in accord with the organic law.

The proposed amendment strongly suggests Mr. Roosevelt's scheme for the recall of judicial decisions, except that the present idea is to make the recall by a vote of Congress, while his suggestion was to submit the matter to a vote of the people. That much more logical and democratic, though equally dangerous, proposition met with no popular acclaim, let alone support, despite the tremendous driving force and prestige of its sponsor, a natural leader of public thought and former President of the United States. The world has been upset since then, however, and times have changed, so we must not take for granted too much common sense or good judgment, when considering what will be the verdict on this latest proposition for a change in our fundamental law.

If the public be fully informed as to the scope and possible effect of the suggested amendment, we need not fear the result; but believers in the present system, particularly those fitted for such a battle, must gird themselves for the great debate which looms on the political horizon. This means acquiring knowledge of the facts involved and giving thought to them. Sneers at those who head the other side will fall far short of winning the fight, for many of them are men of parts, representing a following that will have to be brought over to the right view of the question by the use of reason, and not through ridicule or abuse.

The latest move against the system of judicial review begins, apparently, by conceding that the right to declare acts unconstitutional is established, and then proceeds to confer on Congress power to review the exercise of this judicial function. Thus the opposition would have, for the ultimate judges of the meaning of the Constitution, a constantly changing political body, whose members as a rule are most concerned with matters of the immediate moment, rather than with questions of fundamental law, which affect the life of the whole people today, tomorrow, and for all time to come, and which ought to be decided by trained men, guided by scientific reasoning, removed from motives of political or economic expediency, and possessed of a constant desire to maintain the Constitution. Surely it must prove a grave mistake to substitute, for decisions of a tribunal of impartial legal experts, interpretive conclusions on the meaning of the Constitution reached through political maneuvering or in the heat of forensic debate between men unskilled in judicial analysis and without the peculiar sense of responsibility to the law as a system,—of which the Constitution is the keystone,— that attaches to the judicial office and is always felt by the true judge.

As an indication of the ineffectiveness of a constitutional provision binding on the legislature, but beyond the power of the

courts to enforce, I may cite the require-
ment of the Constitution of Pennsylvania
that "immediately after each United
States decennial census" the "General Assembly shall apportion the state into sen-
atorial and representative districts."
From 1874 to 1921, this provision, notwithstanding its imperative form, was either entirely ignored or only in part com-
plied with. This instance of omission is
significant, as showing the lack of effect
on a normally intelligent legislative body
of constitutional provisions which stand
alone, with no mandate to enforce them.

If the legally enforceable meaning of
all provisions in constitutions is to be subject to the decision of the legislative department as conclusive, it is plain to be
seen that our entire judicial system,—the
jurisdiction, procedure, and power of the
courts, as well as the method of selecting
and impeaching judges,—will exist only so
long as the legislature shall not choose to
alter or abolish it, and, moreover, the constitutional rights of the individual, which an

independent judiciary was intended to
protect against the forbidden actions of a
voting majority, will no longer be safe-
guarded.

We know that the Constitution under-
takes to guarantee to those living in this
country certain liberties, which the framers thought essential to the peace of society and the happiness of the people in general. It was framed and adopted by men
who had lived close to the days of religious
and political persecution, who realized that
such days might come again and that it
was necessary to guard against them by
fundamental laws, which could be changed
only after hot heads had time to cool; so
they laid down certain principles which,
until altered by the deliberate method of
constitutional amendment, should bind all
alike, both majorities and minorities.
Thus they guarded the latter against the
momentary passions and desires of the former.

Among other things, the Constitution
guarantees religious freedom. Should

Congress pass an act, the effect of which would be to give one religious sect recognition denied to another, or take from one sect liberties enjoyed by another, of course the courts would refuse to enforce it, because a violation of the fundamental law. Under the proposed amendment, however, if Congress again passed the act, the courts would be rendered powerless, and religious freedom for all the people would be gone. The right to trial by jury, to own property, and other similar rights which we now take for granted, because guaranteed by the Constitution, might, it is perfectly possible to conceive, be pared down, or denied to particular classes, who happen to be unpopular at given times of agitation; and, if this amendment were adopted, the courts would be without power to protect those affected.

It is not to be supposed that, given free rein, the legislatures would entirely disregard the Constitution. On the contrary, we may reasonably believe that, in ordinary times, the effort would be to abide by the limitations of the organic law; but, in seasons when passionate or thoughtless public feeling has been aroused for some particular object, a legislature or congress, elected on or affected by that cry, would in all probability respond to the call, even though the judicial department had expressed the opinion that the object sought to be accomplished was in conflict with the Constitution.

The real danger is that, with the quick and impulsive—decide-in-haste-and-repent-at-leisure — American national temperament, such a scheme as now advocated would really mean the abolition of the written constitution as a shield to protect the stay-at-home, property-owning, peace-loving, substantial citizen against the momentary passions, beliefs, or desires of a voting majority, seeking to accomplish some object forbidden by the fundamental law. For instance, the federal Constitution provides that persons accused of crime have the right to be tried in the state where the offense was committed. It is

not hard to imagine a condition of affairs
where, in one part of the country, public
sentiment might make the conviction of
those accused of offenses against a certain
national law easy, whereas it might be
quite the reverse in other sections. Suppose, under these conditions, Congress
passed, and, when judicially overruled, re-
passed a law to the effect that those accused of the particular offense in question
should be tried at some central point. If
this course of defying the Constitution in
response to public sentiment were success-
fully pursued in one instance it could, and
in all probability would, be in others; and
very soon, for all practical purposes, we
would cease to live under a constitutional
government, or perhaps in some localities,
under a republican form of government,
which is expressly guaranteed by the Constitution to "every state." In fact, all the
rights which the states refused to delegate
to the federal government could be trans-
ferred to it by ultimate act of Congress.
Freedom of speech, of the press, of our

homes from intrusion by those in authority without a search warrant duly obtained, and many other such rights, also would
at times, be in danger from an unrestrain-
ed legislature, notwithstanding the protection supposed to be afforded them by the
Constitution. If it be said such dangers
are bound to exist even under the system
of judicial review, the answer is that experience has shown the contrary.

The fact that, under our present system,
the judiciary have been able to stand firmly and persistently for the maintenance
of the Constitution, and generally with
public approval, is due, no doubt, to the following causes: First, the courts consist of
men appointed for life or elected for long
terms; second, these men are learned in
the law and, on the average, traditionally
conservative in thought; and, third, they
do not feel themselves licensed by the people to carry out the wishes of the moment.
Then the system affords its own guaranties against abuse. A judicial decision on
a constitutional point owing to the right of

appeal from one tribunal to another is usually considered by several separate and distinct courts, and by many judges, before it finally passes into the law, and, under present methods, before any possible departure from constitutional requirements can pass through legislation into law, it must ordinarily be concurred in by all branches of the government; that is to say, the statute must be enacted by the legislature, approved by the executive, and, if attacked, affirmed by the courts; and, since such concurrence is not likely to be obtained for legislation which conflicts with the organic law, the Constitution is thus amply protected from governmental abuse of power. In cases out of the ordinary, where an executive vetoes a bill as unconstitutional, and, being passed over his veto, it is subsequently sustained by the courts, the constitutional validity of the act is concurred in by at least two departments of the government, the legislative and the judicial, acting with the benefit of the executive's views.

Thus we see that, under the existing system, it usually takes action by all three branches of the government to make into law legislation attacked as unconstitutional, and this can never be done without the concurrence of both the law-making and law-construing departments. Where a difference of opinion as to the organic validity of a particular piece of legislation is shown by the refusal of the courts to follow it, the lawmakers, if they conceive the interests of the public demand the legislation in question, can always, and of their own accord, set going the wheels to bring about an amendment of the Constitution, which will either of itself achieve the desired end, or permit apposite legislation; and, as we said before, if there is a real demand, recent occurrences have shown that the road to such relief is not an over-difficult one to travel.

To all the points just stated, the other side will say: We are not interested in acts sustained; what concerns us are those not sustained; our complaint is that, as to the latter class, the judicial department can overrule both of the other departments. As a matter of fact, however, the courts do not overrule, annul, or veto laws made by the legislature and approved by the executive. What they do is to compare the enactments of the lawmakers with the Constitution, to see whether the former plainly infringes any of the fundamental rules laid down in the latter, and, if in any instance this occurs, the court, in the fulfillment of its duty to judge the law, points out that the legislation in question is not binding, because forbidden by the higher law of the Constitution itself, of which the complainant in the particular case is entitled to the benefit and cannot be deprived by any act of the legislature.[111] It must be kept in mind that constitutional questions, so far as the courts are concerned with

---

[111] Since the delivery of these lectures, Mr. Justice Sutherland has made a significant announcement of the principle above referred to, in the case of Commonwealth of Massachusetts v. Mellon, Secretary of the Treasury, 43 Sup. Ct. 597, 67 L. Ed. ——.

them, arise only in actual litigation, where
one side claims the benefit of a legislative
act and the other the protection of a constitutional provision. If these two are in
plain conflict, the court has to say which is
the law, and obviously, under such circumstances, the decision must be given in favor of the Constitution and against the act.
But, say the opponents of such review,
judges, like legislators, are human, and
may make mistakes, or even abuse their
power. Granting this, as of course we
have to, yet any system of government
must be administered by man, and the judiciary,—the agency selected by common
consent to ascertain and administer the
law,—is better fitted for such work than
any other available.

Another United States Senator [112] is
willing to allow the power of review to
the courts, but he wants to regulate it.
He suggests an act of Congress providing
that at least seven out of the nine members
of the federal Supreme Court must agree

---

[112] Senator Borah; see note 5, supra.

before a statute is declared unconstitutional, which means that, if six of the judges
are convinced beyond doubt a particular
piece of legislation breaches the very letter
of the fundamental law, and three are unwilling to say so, the judgment or attitude
of the three shall prevail; in other words,
that we shall substitute minority for majority rule.

Let us examine some actual cases to
see how the suggested rule might have
worked, had it been in force when these
cases were determined. The Constitution
declares that "no person" shall be held to
answer for an infamous crime, unless on a
presentment of indictment by a grand jury,
nor be deprived of life, liberty, or property,
without due process of law, and that "in
all criminal prosecutions, the accused shall
enjoy the right to a speedy and public trial
by an impartial jury of the state and district wherein the crime shall have been
committed." Notwithstanding these plain
guaranties to all persons in this country,
a federal statute was passed which provid-

ed that certain breaches of the immigration laws, by a special class of foreigners, should be tried summarily before executive officers, and, if the accused were found guilty, he should be "imprisoned at hard labor for a period not exceeding one year, and thereafter removed from the United States." The Supreme Court held the statute unconstitutional; it could not do otherwise. Again, the Constitution guarantees that private property shall not be taken for public use without just compensation being paid or secured to the owner, yet Congress provided for the condemnation of property of a navigation company without paying for one of its most valuable assets, the franchise right to collect tolls. The Supreme Court protected the corporation against this unlawful confiscation by declaring the statute an unconstitutional exercise of power. In these two cases (Wong Wing v. United States, 163 U. S. 228, 16 Sup. Ct. 977, 41 L. Ed. 140; Monongahela Nav. Co. v. United States, 148 U. S. 312, 13 Sup. Ct. 622, 37 L. Ed. 463),

—and many others equally strong could be mentioned,—had the proposition now under discussion been in force, the litigant who stood on his rights as guaranteed by the Constitution, might have been told by the Supreme Court: "Six of us feel that the fundamental law is as you claim it to be, and that the statute pleaded against you infringes that law; but, since three of us feel otherwise (or do not desire to oppose the will of the legislature), the court is powerless to decide in your favor." That is the proposition in a nutshell; how does it appeal to you?

A third proposition largely like the one just discussed has been brought forward by another Senator.[113] His suggestion is that an act of Congress should be voidable by the Supreme Court "only when two-

---

[113] Senator Fess; see note 6, supra. While Senator Fess is against congressional recall of court decisions, or any such change, yet he seems to think the time has come when, in order to save the present system from what may prove destructive attacks, it would be wise to limit or regulate the exercise of the right of judicial review; but the Senator does not state whether this shall be by amendment or congressional action.

thirds of the court concurs, unless upon a case to be confirmed from a lower court, where the unconstitutionality was decreed by at least more than a mere majority vote." This Senator points to several requirements in the Constitution for a two-thirds vote, such as that which provides for the overriding of the President's veto, and, again, the essential vote in impeachment proceedings. The instances cited do not involve the judicial decision of a point of law. They relate to political balloting, according to the representatives' sense of expediency or on the facts of a particular charge,—quite different matters from the registering of a decisive judicial view on the law and applying it to the adjustment or determination of property or personal rights in actual litigation.[114]

---

[114] Warren, in his "Supreme Court in United States History," at page 125, vol. II, states, as to a proposition somewhat similar to the one under discussion, it entirely lost sight of the fact that suits involving the validity of statutes were "litigation between individuals and presented questions of property or personal rights," where each litigant was entitled to equal protection, and therefore any plan which required an appellant to persuade

But suppose the vital difference just pointed out should not be insisted upon. According to our American custom, constitutions may be adopted by a bare majority of a convention called for that purpose or by a majority vote of the people, and the decision of other important questions by such a vote is the general rule. Why depart from this democratic custom? As one of our leading journals,[115] discussing the proposition now under consideration, recently stated editorially: "It would be just as reasonable to insist upon the passage of acts of Congress by a two-thirds vote, instead of a majority, as to insist upon the proposed change of practice in the Supreme Court." To my mind, this would be even more reasonable; but, if there is to be any change in the prevailing system, it must be confessed

---

more than a majority of the court, while the appellee carried a less burden, gave to the latter "in a lawsuit very heavy odds," adding that, under such a scheme parties would not come into court "on an equal basis, but with the chances heavily weighted against an appellant, and this was not in consonance with any Anglo-Saxon system of justice."

[115] Washington Post, April 2, 1923.

that the present suggestion is the least objectionable of those lately advanced.

## XIV.  HOW WELL THE POWER OF JUDICIAL REVIEW HAS BEEN USED

The judicial branch of the government
differs from the executive or legislative
department, in that the former, unlike the
latter, "possesses neither the power of the
purse nor the sword." [116]  Structurally, the
judicial branch is the weakest of the three,
because it must depend for actual physical
power to enforce its mandates on such
force as may be furnished to it by the other
departments.  In spite of this obstacle,
however, the courts, because of the confidence they command, have come to óccu-
py a powerful position in our scheme of
government, which bears witness to a
proper administration, on the whole, of the
high powers entrusted to them.  If they

[116] Com. v. Gamble, 62 Pa. 343, 345–347, 1 Am. Rep.
422.

had failed to win such confidence, history would not record the steady growth in power and prestige of the American judiciary, but quite another story.

That, up to date, the judges have not abused their power in the field under discussion, I think is made manifest by statistics. For example, during the period of its existence, the United States Supreme Court has held unconstitutional only 49 acts of Congress, about 310 acts of state legislatures, and some 42 municipal ordinances.[117]

Statistics quoted by Prof. B. F. Moore, in the Columbia University Historical Studies,[118] indicate that, of the federal statutes questioned before the Supreme Court from 1790 to 1910, less than 18 per cent. were declared invalid, and, when we take into account the fact that only the most vulnerable of such enactments are brought for final judgment before the court of ultimate appeal, this percentage is not high.

---

[117] See tabulations in Addenda, pp. 141, 149, 168, infra.
[118] Vol. LIV, No. 2, p. 141.

Although there may be differences of opinion about the propriety of the decision in some of the cases where the Supreme Court declared acts of Congress unconstitutional, still, when looked at impartially, it cannot be said that an abuse of power appears in any of these cases. Furthermore, when we remember that in 133 years only 49 of the thousands of acts passed have been declared invalid, it cannot be well contended that the power of review has been unduly exercised.

While we have been considering the subject before us largely from the national aspect, and the right of the judiciary to review acts of Congress has been the leading point in mind, yet it may be helpful to see how the general system has worked in one of the oldest and largest of our states.

From 1790 to 1921, the Legislature of Pennsylvania passed approximately 40,-000 acts, of which less than one-half of one per cent have been held to conflict with the organic law; and, in considering this percentage of acts declared invalid, we must remember they had to be compared with constitutions containing an unusually large number of prohibitions and guaranties. For example, in the present Pennsylvania Constitution, adopted in 1874, we find at least 150 express or implied limitations on the right of legislation, many of which are possible of breach in several different ways; this calculation omits provisions regulatory of proceedings in the legislature itself, which, because of their nature, are beyond the scope of judicial review.

Of the acts contested on constitutional grounds in the Supreme Court of Pennsylvania, about four-fifths were sustained and one-fifth declared invalid, a proportion which seems quite small considering the very numerous fundamental inhibitions just noted.

I suppose that the Pennsylvania figures are fairly illustrative of the exercise of the power of review by state courts generally, and, to my mind, they show a conservative use of it; they undoubtedly indicate no abuse.

The exercise of the power within the state is important, in contemplating the proposed changes, as any serious attempt to eliminate, diminish, or control the power of judicial review in our federal system, will almost surely have its effect elsewhere; and, possibly before the innovation had a fair trial in the national field, it would cause similar, if not more radical changes in the fundamental laws of many of the states; hence the questions under discussion must interest us not only as Americans, but as citizens of our several commonwealths.

Critics of the present system point to the fact that, during the period since the first half century of our national existence, there has been a considerable increase in the volume of acts declared unconstitutional; they argue from this that the federal Supreme Court, and probably other tribunals exercising the power of judicial review, have ceased to abide by the limitations of the rule that this power shall be asserted only when an infringement of the Constitution is plain beyond doubt. They also point to the many instances of recent years where acts of Congress have been declared unconstitutional by an almost evenly divided Supreme Court.[119] All appellate courts may well heed both these criticisms, for any tendency to depart from the early rule, that the power to find an act of the legislature unconstitutional should be exercised in clear cases only, will draw upon the judiciary merited resentment; and, when the meaning of the Constitution is before a court for determination, a failure

---

119 An article entitled "Five-to-Four Decisions of the Supreme Court of the United States," 54 American Law Review, 481, by Fred A. Maynard, Esq., contains a list of such decisions, which, when examined and brought down to date, indicates that, in the whole history of the court, this division has existed in but thirty cases where the constitutionality of a state or federal legislative act was involved, and in only eight of these was an enact·ment of Congress declared unconstitutional by a five-to-four vote. With the exception of a short interval, the Supreme Court has consisted of nine members since 1837 Warren, "The Supreme Court in United States History,' vol. II, p. 313; Id., vol. III, p. 223.

on the part of judges constituting the tribunal to make every possible effort to agree is a matter of moment, which calls for consideration by the judiciary itself, since, unless in every case of this character such effort is made, the failure of our courts in that regard will be seriously misunderstood by the public at large, and this misunderstanding may, in the end, affect adversely our political institutions.

As a matter of fact, however, the two criticisms under discussion are largely undeserved; for, while apparently the time which has elapsed since our first half century of national existence, when compared with the earlier period, shows a considerable increase of acts avoided, yet this is readily accounted for by the increase in legislation, brought about by the enormous changes in the physical, industrial, economic, and social conditions of life. The growth of legislation, and the coming of modern facilities of travel and communication, of course had the effect of augmenting appeals in general, and thus raising the total of cases involving constitutional questions. For example, Solicitor General Beck tells that, during Chief Justice Marshall's career of 35 years on the bench, he filed only 528 opinions, including his dissents, less than 15 a year; whereas the present Chief Justice of Pennsylvania writes about 100 a year. This shows the difference in the times. The Solicitor General, in a most interesting address, recently delivered before the Law Academy of Philadelphia, states: Prior to 1825 the federal Supreme Court disposed of an average of 24 cases a year; from 1826 to 1830, the average was 58; and from 1846 to 1850, only 71. This may be compared with the annual average of the last five years, which is over 1,000 cases. The court today does ten times the work it did in Marshall's day, and it may be added that its problems are tenfold more complex. Nearly 800 cases have arisen under the Fourteenth Amendment, and over 200 cases under the commerce clause, during the last 30 years; the Solicitor General thinks it is probably a conservative estimate to say that, in this period, over 1,500 cases involving an interpretation of the Constitution have been argued, in which the question was one of substance.

Considering how very meager was the total of cases heard by the judiciary in the period which marked the beginning of our history, I venture to say that, although the number of acts then declared unconstitutional was few, it represented, nevertheless an exercise of the power with proportionately as great frequency as in the later and present periods, with their endless mass of litigation.[120]

As to the lack of judicial harmony on constitutional questions, the increase in the number of judges constituting our courts of appeal, from three or less in the early times, to seven or nine in these days, with the opportunities for discord which such large courts present, and,—with our

---

[120] See B. F. Moore, "The Courts and Unconstitutional Legislation," 54 Columbia Historical Studies, No. 2, p. 141.

overcrowded court calendars,—the difficulty to find sufficient time for proper consultations, together with the rapidity with which cases of public moment usually are decided, well account for the many failures of our appellate tribunals to present united fronts on constitutional points.

It is frequently argued that where, in considering the validity of legislation, four judges out of nine do not regard the statute as unconstitutional, there cannot be present such a clear infringement of the fundamental law as to warrant the other five in declaring the act void. The answer to this contention is that the opinion of each particular judge voting with the majority relates to a clear and palpable violation of the Constitution, and therefore the view of the five is that the conflict is manifest and unavoidable, an opinion which, under their oaths to support and maintain the Constitution, they are bound to assert,[121] and which, according to our American method of abiding by the legally

121 See Com. v. Hyneman. 242 Pa. 244, 252, 88 Atl. 1015.

expressed view of a majority, should be accepted as controlling.

There is still another way of looking at this matter of dissents: Written constitutions are drawn along broad lines, so that the general principles thus enunciated may comprehend both contemporaneous and future conditions. With this all-important factor in mind, it is not to be wondered at that, when these general principles are to be applied to new conditions, there should arise differences of opinion as to their proper interpretations, or, when that is agreed on, as to their applicability; but divergent views are bound to exist under any system, and surely it is better to have judges, fitted by tradition and training, settle such matters, even if they do insist upon spreading their several opinions on the record, than to have them passed on conclusively by a purely political body, where, no doubt, the differences would be quite as marked, and probably somewhat more vociferously uttered.

Indeed, the deliberate and usually calm

discussion of constitutional questions, which, under our system of judicial review, constantly appears in the public press and law reports, plays a real part in preserving the rules of the fundamental law as living principles of government,—even more, perhaps, than the actual decisions on such questions. These discussions keep the requirements of the Constitution before the people, their legislative representatives, and the judges who preside in the trial courts, and this alone is a most important accomplishment; moreover, they serve to acquaint the world at large with the American doctrine of judicial review, which, it is pleasing to note, has commanded a large degree of foreign approval.

## XV.  ATTITUDE OF MODERN DEMOCRACIES

Our system of judicial review is generally regarded by European publicists as America's chief contribution in the field of political science.   Viscount Bryce, in his "American

Commonwealth," observes that "there is no part of the American system which reflects more credit on its authors or has worked better in practice." Then he goes on to say: "It has had the advantage of relegating questions, not only intricate and delicate, but peculiarly liable to excite political passions, to the cool, dry atmosphere of judicial determination." [122] Professor Dicey advocates judicial review for the British Empire. His book, "The Law of the Constitution," [123] states that "the glory of the founders of the United States is to have devised or adopted arrangements under which the Constitution became in reality as well as in name the supreme law of the land."

Much more such praise might be quoted, but the indorsement of the doctrine does not stop with the writers. [124] We find many

---

[122] Pages 256, 257.

[123] Page 154.

[124] Roscoe Pound, in his "Spirit of the Common Law," states at page 3: "In the reports of South American republics we find judicial discussions of constitutional problems fortified with citation of American authorities. In the South African reports we find a court composed of

modern democracies adopting it as a part of
their political systems. The most notable
example of this is Australia, where the High
Court has persistently maintained the anal-
ogy of the Australian and American Constitutions, and, citing Marbury v. Madison,
has declared invalid legislative acts of the
state and federal governments, though no
express grant of power so to do is contained in the Constitution.[125] In Canada,
both the provincial and Dominion courts
have assumed the right to review legislation, albeit they are obliged to concede that

Dutch judges, trained in the Roman-Dutch law, holding
a legislative act invalid and citing Marbury v. Madison,
—the foundation of American constitutional law,—along
with the modern civilians. The Australian bench and
bar, notwithstanding a decision of the Judicial Committee of the Privy Council of England, are insisting
upon the authority of Australian courts to pass upon
the constitutionality of state statutes, and the Privy
Council has found itself obliged to pronounce invalid a
confiscatory statute enacted by a Canadian province.
Even continental publicists may be found asserting it
a fundamental defect of their public law that constitutional principles are not protected by an independent
court of justice."

[125] Charles G. Haines, "Judicial Interpretation of the
Constitutional Act of the Commonwealth of Australia,"
30 Harvard Law Rev. 595.

the authoritative exposition of the British North American Act rests with the Judicial Committee of the Privy Council in England. Subject to the same right of appeal to the Privy Council, the colonial courts of New Zealand and the South African Republic apply the doctrine of judicial review, and there is even one instance of an Indian court declaring void a legislative act of the Governor General of India in Council.

Outside of the British Empire, the doctrine has been adopted, in a more or less modified form, by Roumania, Argentina, Brazil, Bolivia, Colombia, Cuba, Mexico, and Venezuela. The French Parliament is supreme, even to the extent of amending the Constitution; but Professor Garner tells us [126] in recent years there has developed in that country a decided tendency to extend the power of the judiciary, and, he says, there are many French jurists who

[126] "Judicial Control of Administrative and Legislative Acts in France," American Pol. Sc. Rev. vol. IX, p. 637.

advocate the adoption of the American system. The latest approval of our doctrine is manifested by the new Irish Constitution, which gives the courts power to nullify legislative acts repugnant to the Constitution or the Anglo-Irish treaty, subject, however, to the right of appeal to the English Privy Council.[127]

Thus, although some European countries are loath to abandon parliamentary sovereignty, the fact seems beyond dispute that the democracies of the world are fast coming to see both sound principle and the practicalities of the situation require that a recognized body, removed from the momentary influences of political atmosphere, be given the right of passing on the constitutionality of statutes, whenever a legislature is restricted in its powers by the provisions of a written fundamental law. Who better than the courts can be trusted with this very important power, affecting, as it does, the stability of the state, and the life, liberty and

---

[127] Philadelphia Public Ledger, June 16, 1922.

prosperity of the people? What man, when he stops to consider the matter, would not rather trust the solution of questions of fundamental law affecting his rights, and the rights and happiness of all the people, to the trained judge, in his environment, rather than to the untrained legislator, influenced as he is, and must be, by the expediencies of the moment and political motives? Why should we surrender that which has not only met with the approbation of many of the best thinkers in other parts of the world, but also, because of its success with us, with actual adoption by many other countries?

## XVI. FINAL THOUGHTS

Before concluding, let me remind you that all judges necessarily incur a degree of unpopularity, for one side always loses in every case, and, as constitutions are drawn largely to protect the human, political, and property rights of minorities from the temporary desires of majorities, it stands to reason that, in upholding and enforcing these rights, the courts are frequently called on to render decisions which, at least for the time being, do not command general sup‧ port; but, making allowances for this, when an impartial observer considers the momentous changes which have occurred in all departments of life since the beginning of our national existence and the mass of legislation which has accompanied them, he must be impressed with the thought that, on the whole, the great power vested in the judiciary has been well and temperately administered. It seems to me this is shown by the figures I have quoted.

It is not surprising that a few mistakes, or even abuses of power, have crept in; the only surprising thing is that more cannot justifiably be pointed to. I know, by almost twenty years of experience on the bench, that even today, when the right is established, judges, as a rule, look upon the power to review legislation with a sense of grave responsibility, and adhere closely to what has

become a fixed principle, that such authority
shall never be exercised unless a case of palpable violation of the Constitution is made to
appear. The controlling rule is plainly stated in a recent opinion of the Supreme Court
of Pennsylvania [128] thus: "The power of the
judiciary to declare void a legislative enactment which contravenes the organic law, is
established, but this is subject to the restric-
tion that no court has the right to exercise
such power unless the legislation attacked
so plainly violates some mandate of the
Constitution that it cannot be sustained under any reasonable construction; it is the
duty of every judge, without regard to his
opinion as to the necessity for or the wisdom
of the act of assembly before him, to search
for a construction which will support the legislative interpretation of the Constitution,
and an act can never properly be declared
void unless this is found to be impossible."
That this rule has been well observed is dem-

---

[128] Com. v. Hyneman, 242 Pa. 244, 263, 264, 88 Atl.
1015.

onstrated by the few instances of acts declared invalid when compared with the mass of legislation enacted, as one may see by a study of the facts; and I have no doubt that, when these facts are placed clearly before the public, the electorate will reject any attack on the power under discussion, or proposition to transfer it elsewhere.

We of this generation have had more than our share of mechanical and scientific advancement, but of what political discovery or achievement can we boast which warrants us in taking the risk of uprooting the work of our ancestors, who, so far as the making of governmental institutions is concerned, lived in one of the finest periods of formative political thought?

Within the last year or so, the people of at least three of our greatest commonwealths (New York, Pennsylvania, and Illinois) have declined, by considerable majorities, to intrust representatives with power to draft new state constitutions, even though these representatives were to be elected for the purpose, and their work would, in the end, have to be voted on and adopted by the people themselves, or, where such drafts have been made, the people have refused, by large majorities, to accept them; yet it is seriously suggested that we shall cut into the organic law of the nation and vest the federal legislature with power, in effect, to amend the Constitution at will, without any referendum on the subject. The people, unwilling at this time to trust themselves, or their representatives specially selected for the purpose, with the rewriting of state constitutions, must be brought to see the dangerous comprehensiveness of the newly suggested plan whereby their general representatives in Congress are to be empowered to overrule the Supreme Court and thus, from time to time, to remake the national Constitution.

Schemes of liberal government are devised to serve the best interests of all concerned, and any system which has administered to the mass-happiness of a people, by enabling them to live together for a long period in comparative peace, harmony and prosperity, should not be tinkered with for the sake of an experiment, which not only holds forth no prospect of bettering conditions, but is fraught with dangers, to the continued existence of our constitutional structure, greater than any conceivable in the plan under which we are now working.

If a remedy is needed, so far as the federal Supreme Court is concerned, the real one would be to restrict the appellate jurisdiction of that overburdened tribunal, confining it largely to the consideration of appeals involving constitutional questions, and thus allow sufficient time to examine into, confer upon, and, where possible, to reconcile differences on, these most important points; then let the liberalizing tendencies of the present age work their own way under our existing system, as they are steadily doing.

Efforts to bring about radical departures from the prevailing system are promised, however, and a desire to assist in preventing possibly fatal misunderstandings concerning the real nature of the American doctrine of judicial review, its historic antecedents, and the facts attending its exercise, led me to undertake the preparation of these lectures, which I trust will prove helpful in dispelling some of the mistaken teachings and beliefs of the present day.

\*

# ADDENDUM I

## UNITED STATES
## SUPREME COURT DECISIONS
### DECLARING
## FEDERAL LEGISLATION UNCONSTI-
## TUTIONAL

NOTE.—The following list has been prepared from an examination of four sources: (1) That published by Congress in 1889, appearing in appendix of Volume 131, U. S. Reports; (2) a list (1789–1910) compiled by Prof. Blaine F. Moore, in Columbia Historical Studies, Vol. LIV, No. 2, page 129; (3) a list furnished by the Clerk of the United States Supreme Court; and (4) a list furnished by the Library of Congress. The acts of Congress involved in each case are cited.

## LIST

United States v. Todd, 13 How. 51 note, 14 L. Ed. 47. Act March 23, 1792; 1 Stat. 243.[1]

---

[1] A note, "inserted by order of the court," to U. S. v. Ferreira, 13 How. 51, 53, 14 L. Ed. 42, states that "the result of the opinions expressed by the judges of the Supreme Court" in U. S. v. Todd was that the act of

Marbury v. Madison, 1 Cranch, 137, 2 L. Ed. 60. Act September 24, 1789, last subsection of section 13; 1 Stat. 81.

Scott v. Sandford, 19 How. 393, 15 L. Ed. 691. Act March 6, 1820, § 8; 3 Stat. 548.

Gordon v. United States, 2 Wall. 561, 77 L. Ed. 921; 117 U. S. 697, Append. Act March 3, 1863; 12 Stat. 765.

Ex parte Garland, 4 Wall. 333, 18 L. Ed. 366. Act January 24, 1865; 13 Stat. 424.

Reichert v. Felps, 6 Wall. 160, 18 L. Ed. 849. Act February 20, 1812; 2 Stat. 677.

The Alicia, 7 Wall. 571, 19 L. Ed. 84. Act June 30, 1864, § 13; 13 Stat. 310.

Hepburn v. Griswold, 8 Wall. 603, 19 L. Ed. 513. Legal Tender Acts of 1862–63; 12 Stat. 345, 532, 709.

---

1792 was "unconstitutional." We include the Todd Case on the authority of this note, despite the fact that writers of authority, such as Professors Thayer, Farrand, and Haines, question whether the decision actually rested on the constitutional point. See Haines, "The American Doctrine of Judicial Supremacy," p. 159.

United States v. De Witt, 9 Wall. 41, 19 L. Ed. 593. Act March 2, 1867, § 29; 14 Stat. 484.

Justices of Supreme Court v. Murray, 9 Wall. 274, 19 L. Ed. 658. Act March 3, 1863, § 5; 12 Stat. 756.

Collector v. Day, 11 Wall. 113, 20 L. Ed. 122. Income Tax Acts, 1864–1865– 1866–1867; 13 Stat. 281, 479; 14 Stat. 137, 477.

United States v. Klein, 13 Wall. 128, 20 L. Ed. 519. Act July 12, 1870; 16 Stat. 235.

United States v. Baltimore & O. Ry. Co., 17 Wall. 322, 21 L. Ed. 597. Internal Revenue Act of 1864, § 122, as amended by Act July 13, 1866; 14 Stat. 98, 138.

United States v. Reese, 92 U. S. 214, 23 L. Ed. 563. Act May 31, 1870; 16 Stat. 140.

United States v. Fox, 95 U. S. 670, 24 L. Ed. 538. R. S. § 5132, subsec. 9.

Trade-Mark Cases, 100 U. S. 82, 25 L. Ed. 550. R. S. §§ 4937–4947.

United States v. Harris, 106 U. S. 629, 1 Sup. Ct. 601, 27 L. Ed. 290. R. S. § 5519.[2]

Civil Rights Cases, 109 U. S. 3, 3 Sup. Ct. 18, 27 L. Ed. 835. Act March 1, 1875, §§ 1, 2; 18 Stat. 336. See, also, Butts v. Transportation Co., infra.

Boyd v. United States, 116 U. S. 616, 6 Sup. Ct. 524, 29 L. Ed. 746. Act June 22, 1874, § 5; 18 Stat. 187.

Callan v. Wilson, 127 U. S. 540, 8 Sup. Ct. 1301, 32 L. Ed. 223. R. S. D. C. § 1064.

Counselman v. Hitchcock, 142 U. S. 547, 12 Sup. Ct. 195, 35 L. Ed. 1110. R. S. § 860.

Monongahela Navigation Co. v. United States, 148 U. S. 312, 13 Sup. Ct. 622, 37 L. Ed. 463. Act August 11, 1888; 25 Stat. 411.

Pollock v. Farmers' Loan & Trust Co., 157 U. S. 429, 15 Sup. Ct. 673, 39 L. Ed. 759; 158 U. S. 601, 15 Sup. Ct. 912,

[2] Affirmed in Baldwin v. Franks, 120 U. S. 678, 7 Sup. Ct. 656, 763, 30 L. Ed. 766.

39 L. Ed. 1108. Act August 27, 1894,
§§ 27–37; 28 Stat. 553.

Wong Wing v. United States, 163 U. S.
228, 16 Sup. Ct. 977, 41 L. Ed. 140.
Act May 5, 1892, § 4; 27 Stat. 25.

Kirby v. United States, 174 U. S. 47, 19
Sup. Ct. 574, 43 L. Ed. 809. Act
March 3, 1875; 18 Stat. 479.

Fairbank v. United States, 181 U. S. 283,
21 Sup. Ct. 648, 45 L. Ed. 862. Act
June 13, 1898; 30 Stat. 459, 462.

James v. Bowman, 190 U. S. 127, 23 Sup.
Ct. 678, 47 L. Ed. 979. R. S. § 5507.

Matter of Heff, 197 U. S. 488, 25 Sup.
Ct. 506, 49 L. Ed. 848. Act January
30, 1897; 29 Stat. 506.

Rassmussen v. United States, 197 U. S.
516, 25 Sup. Ct. 514, 49 L. Ed. 862.
Act June 6, 1900, § 171; 31 Stat. 358.

Hodges v. United States, 203 U. S. 1, 27
Sup. Ct. 6, 51 L. Ed. 65. R. S. § 1977.

Employers Liability Cases, 207 U. S. 463,
28 Sup. Ct. 141, 52 L. Ed. 297. Act
June 11, 1906; 34 Stat. 232.

Adair v. United States, 208 U. S. 161, 28 Sup. Ct. 277, 52 L. Ed. 436, 13 Ann. Cas. 764. Act June 1, 1898; 30 Stat. 428.

Keller v. United States, 213 U. S. 138, 29 Sup. Ct. 470, 53 L. Ed. 737, 16 Ann. Cas. 1066; Act February 20, 1907, § 3; 34 Stat. 899.

United States v. Evans, 213 U. S. 297, 29 Sup. Ct. 507, 53 L. Ed. 803. Code, D. C. § 935.

Muskrat v. United States, 219 U. S. 346, 31 Sup. Ct. 250, 55 L. Ed. 246. Act March 1, 1907; 34 Stat. 1028.

Coyle v. Oklahoma, 221 U. S. 559, 31 Sup. Ct. 688, 55 L. Ed. 853. Act June 16, 1906; 34 Stat. 267, c. 3335.

Butts v. Merchants' & Miners' Trans. Co., 230 U. S. 126, 33 Sup. Ct. 964, 57 L. Ed. 1422. Act March 1, 1875, §§ 1, 2; 18 Stat. 336.

United States v. Hvoslef, 237 U. S. 1, 35 Sup. Ct. 459, 59 L. Ed. 813, Ann. Cas.

1916A, 286. Act June 13, 1898; 30 Stat. 460.

Thames & Mersey Marine Ins. Co. v. United States, 237 U. S. 19, 35 Sup. Ct. 496, 59 L. Ed. 821, Ann. Cas. 1915D, 1087. Act June 13, 1898, c. 448; 30 Stat. 448, 461.

Hammer v. Dagenhart, 247 U. S. 251, 38 Sup. Ct. 529, 62 L. Ed. 1101, 3 A. L. R. 649, Ann. Cas. 1918E, 724. Act September 1, 1916; 39 Stat. 675, 676.

Eisner v. Macomber, 252 U. S. 189, 40 Sup. Ct. 189, 64 L. Ed. 521, 9 A. L. R. 1570. Act September 8, 1916, c. 463; 39 Stat. 756.

Knickbocker Ice Co. v. Stewart, 253 U. S. 149, 40 Sup. Ct. 438, 64 L. Ed. 834, 11 A. L. R. 1145. Act October 6, 1917; 40 Stat. 395.

Evans v. Gore, 253 U. S. 245, 40 Sup. Ct. 550, 64 L. Ed. 887, 11 A. L. R. 519. Act February 24, 1919, § 213; 40 Stat. 1065.

United States v. L. Cohen Grocery Co.,
255 U. S. 81, 41 Sup. Ct. 298, 65 L. Ed.
516, 14 A. L. R. 1045. Act August 10,
1917, c. 53, § 4; 40 Stat. 276; amended
Act October 22, 1919, c. 80, § 2; 41
Stat. 297.

Newberry v. United States, 256 U. S. 232,
41 Sup. Ct. 469, 65 L. Ed. 913. Act
June 25, 1910, c. 392; 36 Stat. 822;
amended Act August 19, 1911, c. 33;
37 Stat. 25.

United States v. Moreland, 258 U. S. 433,
42 Sup. Ct. 368, 66 L. Ed. 700. Act
March 23, 1906; 34 Stat. 86, c. 1131.

Bailey v. Drexel Furniture Co., 259 U. S.
20, 42 Sup. Ct. 449, 66 L. Ed. 817, 21
A. L. R. 1432. Title 12, Act February
24, 1919; 40 Stat. 1057, 1138.

Hill v. Wallace, 259 U. S. 44, 42 Sup. Ct.
453, 66 L. Ed. 822. Act August 24,
1921; 42 Stat. 187.

Adkins v. Children's Hospital of the District of Columbia, 43 Sup. Ct. 394, 67 L.
Ed. ——. Act September 19, 1918; 40
Stat. 960, c. 174.

# ADDENDUM II

---

## UNITED STATES
## SUPREME COURT DECISIONS
### DECLARING
## STATE LEGISLATION UNCONSTITU-
## TIONAL

---

Note.—The succeeding lists cover United States Supreme Court Reports, Vols. 221–256, and Vol. 257 to page 311. For Vols. 1–220, see Prof. Blaine F. Moore, "The Supreme Court and Unconstitutional Legislation," Columbia Historical Studies, Vol. LIV, No. 2, Appendix II. The act, or section of a statute, affected by each decision is given wherever possible. The meaning of a letter standing before any case is explained by reference to the following table:

a. State statute held inoperative because superseded by a United States statute, which Congress had authority to enact.

b. Territorial statute, violating an organic act passed by Congress.

c. State Constitution and statute.

d. State statute violative of state Constitution.

e. State Constitution and municipal ordinance.

## LIST

Oklahoma v. Kansas Natural Gas Co., 221 U. S. 229, 31 Sup. Ct. 564, 55 L. Ed. 716, 35 L. R. A. (N. S.) 1193. Oklahoma Laws 1907, c. 67.[1]

**b.** Berryman v. Board of Trustees of Whitman College, 222 U. S. 334, 32 Sup. Ct. 147, 56 L. Ed. 225. Washington Terr. Laws 1883, p. 399.

**a.** Northern Pacific Ry. Co. v. Washington ex rel. Atkinson, 222 U. S. 370, 32 Sup. Ct. 160, 56 L. Ed. 237. Washington Laws 1907, c. 20.

**a.** Southern Ry. Co. v. Reid & Beam, 222 U. S. 424, 32 Sup. Ct. 140, 56 L. Ed. 257, and 222 U. S. 444, 32 Sup. Ct. 145, 56 L. Ed. 263. North Carolina Rev. 1905, § 2631.[2]

---

[1] The finding of unconstitutionality in this case was reaffirmed in Haskell v. Kansas Natural Gas Co., 224 U. S. 217, 32 Sup. Ct. 442, 56 L. Ed. 738.

[2] The same statute was again held invalid in Southern Ry. Co. v. Burlington Lumber Co., 225 U. S. 99, 32 Sup. Ct. 657, 56 L. Ed. 1001.

**a.** Second Employers' Liability Cases (No. 170) 223 U. S. 1, 53, 55, 32 Sup. Ct. 169, 56 L. Ed. 327, 38 L. R. A. (N. S.) 44. Montana laws.[3]

Louisville & Nashville R. R. v. F. W. Cook Brewing Co., 223 U. S. 70, 32

---

[3] The ruling here made, to the effect that the Congressional regulations on employer's liability supersede state laws, in so far as the former cover the same field as the latter, has been frequently reaffirmed and followed in other cases, where the federal law was applied as against the superseded state statute. See St. Louis, I. M. & S. Ry. v. Hesterly, 228 U. S. 702, 33 Sup. Ct. 703, 57 L. Ed. 1031; St. Louis, S. F. & T. R. Co. v. Seale, 229 U. S. 156, 33 Sup. Ct. 651, 57 L. Ed. 1129, Ann. Cas. 1914C, 156; North Carolina R. Co. v. Zachary, 232 U. S. 248, 34 Sup. Ct. 305, 58 L. Ed. 591, Ann. Cas. 1914C, 159; Taylor v. Taylor, 232 U. S. 363, 34 Sup. Ct. 350, 58 L. Ed. 638; Seaboard Air Line Ry. v. Horton, 233 U. S. 492, 34 Sup. Ct. 635, 58 L. Ed. 1062, L. R. A. 1915C, 1, Ann. Cas. 1915B, 475; Toledo R. R. Co. v. Slavin, 236 U. S. 454, 35 Sup. Ct. 306, 59 L. Ed. 671. It is beyond the power of a state to interfere with the operation of the federal acts. New York Cent. R. Co. v. Winfield, 244 U. S. 147, 37 Sup. Ct. 546, 61 L. Ed. 1045, L. R. A. 1918C, 439, Ann. Cas. 1917D, 1139; Erie R. Co. v. Winfield, 244 U. S. 170, 37 Sup. Ct. 556, 61 L. Ed. 1057, Ann. Cas. 1918B, 662; New Orleans & N. E. R. Co. v. Scarlet, 249 U. S. 528, 39 Sup. Ct. 369, 63 L. Ed. 752; Yazoo & M. V. R. Co. v. Mullins, 249 U. S. 531, 39 Sup. Ct. 368, 63 L. Ed. 754.

Sup. Ct. 189, 56 L. Ed. 355. Kentucky Stat. 1909, § 2569a.[4]

Atchison, Topeka & Santa Fé Ry. v. O'Connor, 223 U. S. 280, 32 Sup. Ct. 216, 56 L. Ed. 436, Ann. Cas. 1913C, 1050. Colorado Laws 1907, c. 211.

Meyer v. Wells Fargo & Co., 223 U. S. 298, 32 Sup. Ct. 218, 56 L. Ed. 445. Oklahoma Laws 1910, c. 44, p. 65.

St. Louis, I. M. & S. Ry. v. Wynne, 224 U. S. 354, 32 Sup. Ct. 493, 56 L. Ed. 799, 42 L. R. A. (N. S.) 102. Arkansas Laws 1907, Act No. 61.

Buck Stove & Range Co. v. Vickers, 226 U. S. 205, 33 Sup. Ct. 41, 57 L. Ed. 189. Kansas Gen. Stat. 1905, § 1358.

a. Chicago, R. I. & Pac. R. Co. v. Hardwick Farmers' Elevator Co., 226 U. S. 426, 33 Sup. Ct. 174, 57 L. Ed. 284, 46 L. R. A. (N. S.) 203. Minnesota Laws 1907, c. 23.

---

[4] This decision was reaffirmed in Adams Express Co. v. Kentucky, 238 U. S. 190, 35 Sup. Ct. 824, 59 L. Ed. 1267, L. R. A. 1916C, 273, Ann. Cas. 1915D, 1167.

**a.** Adams Express Co. v. Croninger, 226 U. S. 491, 33 Sup. Ct. 148, 57 L. Ed. 314, 44 L. R. A. (N. S.) 257. Kentucky statute.[5]

St. Louis, I. M. & S. Ry. Co. v. Edwards, 227 U. S. 265, 33 Sup. Ct. 262, 57 L. Ed. 506. Arkansas Laws 1907, No. 193, p. 457.

Crenshaw v. Arkansas, 227 U. S. 389, 33 Sup. Ct. 294, 57 L. Ed. 565. Arkansas Laws 1909, No. 97, p. 292.[6]

**a.** McDermott v. Wisconsin, 228 U. S. 115, 33 Sup. Ct. 431, 57 L. Ed. 754, 47 L. R. A. (N. S.) 984, Ann. Cas. 1915A, 39. Wisconsin Laws 1907, c. 557.

Ettor v. Tacoma, 228 U. S. 148, 33 Sup. Ct. 428, 57 L. Ed. 773. Washington Laws 1909, c. 80, p. 151.

---

[5] The Carmack Amendment was similarly held to supersede existing state laws in Chicago, B. & Q. Ry. v. Miller, 226 U. S. 513, 33 Sup. Ct. 155, 57 L. Ed. 323; Chicago, S. P., M. & O. R. Co. v. Latta, 226 U. S. 519, 33 Sup. Ct. 155, 57 L. Ed. 328; Missouri, K. & T. Ry. Co. v. Harriman, 227 U. S. 657, 33 Sup. Ct. 397, 57 L. Ed. 690.

[6] The same statute was again held invalid in Rogers v. Arkansas, 227 U. S. 401, 33 Sup. Ct. 298, 57 L. Ed. 569.

Missouri Pac. Ry. Co. v. Tucker, 230 U. S. 340, 33 Sup. Ct. 961, 57 L. Ed. 1507. Kansas Laws 1905, c. 353, p. 589.

Kener v. La Grange Mills, 231 U. S. 215, 34 Sup. Ct. 83, 58 L. Ed. 189. Georgia Constitution.[7]

Chicago, M. & S. P. R. Co. v. Polt, 232 U. S. 165, 34 Sup. Ct. 301, 58 L. Ed. 554. South Dakota Laws 1907, c. 215.[8]

Harrison v. St. Louis & S. F. R. Co., 232 U. S. 318, 34 Sup. Ct. 333, 58 L. Ed. 621, L. R. A. 1915F, 1187. Oklahoma Laws May 26, 1908, House Bill No. 131 (Laws 1908; c. 16, art. 4).

Foote & Co. v. Maryland, 232 U. S. 494, 34 Sup. Ct. 377, 58 L. Ed. 698. Maryland Laws 1910, c. 413.

Farmers' & Mechanics' Sav. Bank of Minneapolis v. Minnesota, 232 U. S.

---

[7] Reaffirms the invalidity of a section of the Georgia Constitution found unconstitutional in Gunn v. Barry, 15 Wall. 610, 21 L. Ed. 212.

[8] The same statute was again held invalid in Chicago, M. & S. P. Ry. Co. v. Kennedy, 232 U. S. 626, 34 Sup. Ct. 463, 58 L. Ed. 762.

516, 34 Sup. Ct. 354, 58 L. Ed. 706.
Minnesota Laws 1907, c. 328.

Stewart v. Michigan, 232 U. S. 665, 34
Sup. Ct. 476, 58 L. Ed. 786. Michigan Comp. Laws 1897, c. 136.

e. Russell v. Sebastian, 233 U. S. 195, 34
Sup. Ct. 517, 58 L. Ed. 912, L. R. A.
1918E, 882, Ann. Cas. 1914C, 1282.
California Const. 1879, art. XI, § 19,
as amended.

Carondelet Canal & Navigation Co. v.
Louisiana, 233 U. S. 362, 34 Sup. Ct.
627, 58 L. Ed. 1001. Louisiana Laws
1906, No. 161.

Smith v. Texas, 233 U. S. 630, 34 Sup.
Ct. 681, 58 L. Ed. 1129, L. R. A.
1915D, 677, Ann. Cas. 1915D, 420.
Texas Laws 1909, c. 46.

a. Erie R. Co. v. New York, 233 U. S. 671,
34 Sup. Ct. 756, 58 L. Ed. 1149, 52 L.
R. A. (N. S.) 266, Ann. Cas. 1915D,
138. New York Laws 1907, c. 627.

c. International Harvester Co. v. Kentucky,
234 U. S. 216, 34 Sup. Ct. 853, 58 L.
Ed. 1284. Kentucky Laws May 20,

1890, Carroll's Ky. St. §§ 3915, 3941a; Kentucky Const. § 198; Laws 1906, c. 117, p. 429; Laws 1908, c. 8, p. 38.[9]

Missouri Pac. Ry. v. Larabee, 234 U. S. 459, 34 Sup. Ct. 979, 58 L. Ed. 1398. Kansas Gen. Stat. 1909, § 6319.

Western Union Tel. Co. v. Brown, 234 U. S. 542, 34 Sup. Ct. 955, 58 L. Ed. 1457. South Carolina Civ. Code 1902, § 2223.

United States v. Reynolds, 235 U. S. 133, 35 Sup. Ct. 86, 59 L. Ed. 162. Alabama Code 1907, §§ 6846, 7632.

Sioux Remedy Co. v. Cope, 235 U. S. 197, 35 Sup. Ct. 57, 59 L. Ed. 193. South Dakota Rev. Code, 1903, §§ 883–885.

Choctaw, O. & G. R. Co. v. Harrison, 235 U. S. 292, 35 Sup. Ct. 27, 59 L. Ed. 234. Oklahoma Laws 1908, p. 640.

---

[9] The constitutional ruling in this case was reaffirmed and followed in International Harvester Co v. Kentucky, 234 U. S. 589, 34 Sup. Ct. 947, 58 L. Ed. 1484, Collins v. Kentucky, 234 U. S. 634, 34 Sup. Ct. 924, 58 L. Ed. 1510, and American Seeding Mach. Co. v. Kentucky, 236 U. S. 660, 35 Sup. Ct. 456, 59 L. Ed. 773.

Coppage v. Kansas, 236 U. S. 1, 35 Sup. Ct. 240, 59 L. Ed. 441, L. R. A. 1915C, 960. Kansas Laws 1903, c. 222.

Heyman v. Hays, 236 U. S. 178, 35 Sup. Ct. 403, 59 L. Ed. 527. Tennessee Laws 1909, c. 479.

**a.** Globe Bank & Trust Co. of Paducah, Ky., v. Martin, 236 U. S. 288, 35 Sup. Ct. 377, 59 L. Ed. 583. Carroll's Kentucky Stat. 1909, § 1907.

**a.** Southern R. Co. v. Indiana Railroad Commission, 236 U. S. 439, 35 Sup. Ct. 304, 59 L. Ed. 661. Indiana statute.

Kirmeyer v. Kansas, 236 U. S. 568, 35 Sup. Ct. 419, 59 L. Ed. 721. Kansas statute.

Northern Pac. Ry. Co. v. North Dakota, 236 U. S. 585, 35 Sup. Ct. 429, 59 L. Ed. 735, L. R. A. 1917F, 1148, Ann. Cas. 1916A, 1. North Dakota Laws 1907, c. 51.

Norfolk & West R. Co. v. West Virginia, 236 U. S. 605, 35 Sup. Ct. 437, 59 L. Ed. 745. West Virginia Laws 1907, c. 41.

Wright v. Central of Georgia Ry., 236 U. S. 674, 35 Sup. Ct. 471, 59 L. Ed. 781. Georgia laws.[10]

Davis v. Virginia, 236 U. S. 697, 35 Sup. Ct. 479, 59 L. Ed. 795, Virginia statute.

Riverside & Dan River Cotton Mills v. Menefee, 237 U. S. 189, 35 Sup. Ct. 579, 59 L. Ed. 910. North Carolina statute.

Chicago, B. & Q. R. Co. v. Wisconsin Railroad Commission, 237 U. S. 220, 35 Sup. Ct. 560, 59 L. Ed. 926. Wisconsin Laws 1911, § 1801.

Coe v. Armour Fertilizer Works, 237 U. S. 413, 35 Sup. Ct. 625, 59 L. Ed. 1027. Florida Gen. Stat. 1906, § 2677, as amended by Laws 1909, c. 5892.

Charleston & W. C. R. Co. v. Varnville Furniture Co., 237 U. S. 597, 35 Sup. Ct. 715, 59 L. Ed. 1137, Ann. Cas. 1916D, 333. South Carolina Civ. Code 1912, § 2573.

---

[10] This decision was reaffirmed and followed in Wright v. Louisville & N. R. Co., 236 U. S. 687, 35 Sup. Ct. 475, 59 L. Ed. 788.

Atchison, T. & S. F. R. Co. v. Vosburg, 238 U. S. 56, 35 Sup. Ct. 675, 59 L. Ed. 1199, L. R. A. 1915E, 953. Kansas Laws 1905, c. 345.

Rossi v. Pennsylvania, 238 U. S. 62, 35 Sup. Ct. 677, 59 L. Ed. 1201. Pennsylvania Laws 1887, p. 113, § 15.

Guinn v. United States, 238 U. S. 347, 35 Sup. Ct. 926, 59 L. Ed. 1340, L. R. A. 1916A, 1124. Oklahoma Constitution, amendment of 1910 to article III, § 4a.

Myers v. Anderson, 238 U. S. 368, 35 Sup. Ct. 932, 59 L. Ed. 1349. Maryland Laws 1908, c. 525, p. 347.

Southwestern Telegraph & Telephone Co. v. Danaher, 238 U. S. 482, 35 Sup. Ct. 886, 59 L. Ed. 1419, L. R. A. 1916A, 1208. Arkansas Kirby's Dig. § 7948.

Chicago, M. & S. P. R. Co. v. Wisconsin, 238 U. S. 491, 35 Sup. Ct. 869, 59 L. Ed. 1423, L. R. A. 1916A, 1133. Wisconsin Laws 1911, c. 272.

Truax v. Raich, 239 U. S. 33, 36 Sup. Ct. 7, 60 L. Ed. 131, L. R. A. 1916D, 545,

Ann. Cas. 1917B, 283. Arizona Laws 1915, p. 12.

Provident Sav. Life Assur. Soc. v. Kentucky, 239 U. S. 103, 36 Sup. Ct. 34, 60 L. Ed. 167, L. R. A. 1916C, 572. Kentucky Stat. 1906, § 4226.

d. Johnson v. Wells Fargo & Co., 239 U. S. 234, 36 Sup. Ct. 62, 60 L. Ed. 243. South Dakota Laws 1907, c. 64, as amended by Laws 1909, c. 162.

Rosenberger v. Pacific Express Co., 241 U. S. 48, 36 Sup. Ct. 510, 60 L. Ed. 880. Texas Laws 1907.

McFarland v. American Sugar Refining Co., 241 U. S. 79, 36 Sup. Ct. 498, 60 L. Ed. 899. Louisiana Laws Extra Session 1915, No. 10.

Wisconsin v. Philadelphia & Reading Coal & Iron Co., 241 U. S. 329, 36 Sup. Ct. 563, 60 L. Ed. 1027. Wisconsin Laws June 20, 1905, § 1770f.

Detroit United Ry. v. Michigan, 242 U. S. 238, 37 Sup. Ct. 87, 61 L. Ed. 268. Michigan Local Acts 1905, p. 1144; Local Acts 1907, p. 940.

McDonald v. Mabee, 243 U. S. 90, 37
Sup. Ct. 343, 61 L. Ed. 608, L. R. A.
1917F, 458. Texas statute.

Rowland v. Boyle, 244 U. S. 106, 37 Sup.
Ct. 577, 61 L. Ed. 1022. Arkansas
Laws 1907.

Southern Pacific Co. v. Jensen, 244 U. S.
205, 37 Sup. Ct. 524, 61 L. Ed. 1086,
L. R. A. 1918C, 451, Ann. Cas. 1917E,
900. New York Consolidated Laws, c.
67, as amended by Laws 1914, cc. 41
and 316.[11]

Seaboard Air Line Ry. v. Blackwell, 244
U. S. 310, 37 Sup. Ct. 640, 61 L. Ed.
1160, L. R. A. 1917F, 1184. Georgia
Civ. Code 1910, §§ 2675–2677.

Western Oil Refining Co. v. Lipscomb,
244 U. S. 346, 37 Sup. Ct. 623, 61 L.
Ed. 1181. Tennessee Laws 1909, c.
479, § 4.

Adams v. Tanner, 244 U. S. 590, 37 Sup.
Ct. 662, 61 L. Ed. 1336, L. R. A. 1917F,

---

[11] This decision was followed in Clyde S. S. Co. v.
Walker, 244 U. S. 255, 37 Sup. Ct. 545, 61 L. Ed. 1116, and
the ruling applied to a Louisiana statute in Peters v.
Veasey, 251 U. S. 121, 40 Sup. Ct. 65, 64 L. Ed. 180.

1163, Ann. Cas. 1917D, 973.  Washington Laws 1915, c. 1.

a. American Express Co. v. South Dakota ex rel. Caldwell, 244 U. S. 617, 37 Sup. Ct. 656, 61 L. Ed. 1352.  South Dakota Laws 1911, c. 207, § 10, as amended by Laws 1913, c. 304.

Looney v. Crane Co., 245 U. S. 178, 38 Sup. Ct. 85, 62 L. Ed. 230.  Texas statute.

Crew Levick Co. v. Pennsylvania, 245 U. S. 292, 38 Sup. Ct. 126, 62 L. Ed. 295. Pennsylvania Laws 1899, p. 184.

International Paper Co. v. Massachusetts, 246 U. S. 135, 38 Sup. Ct. 292, 62 L. Ed. 624, Ann. Cas. 1918C, 617.  Massachusetts Stats. 1909, c. 490, part III, § 56, as amended by Stat. 1914, c. 724, § 1.[12]

New York Life Ins. Co. v. Dodge, 246 U. S. 357, 38 Sup. Ct. 337, 62 L. Ed. 772, Ann. Cas. 1918E, 593.  Missouri Rev. Stat. 1899, § 7897.

---

[12] This ruling was reaffirmed in Locomobile Co. of America v. Massachusetts, 246 U. S. 146, 38 Sup. Ct. 298 62 L. Ed. 631.

McGinis v. California, 247 U. S. 91, 38 Sup. Ct. 440, 62 L. Ed. 999; Id., 247 U. S. 95, 38 Sup. Ct. 441, 62 L. Ed. 1002. California Stats. 1913, c. 342, p. 692.

Georgia v. Trustees of Cincinnati Southern Ry. Co., 248 U. S. 26, 39 Sup. Ct. 14, 63 L. Ed. 104. Georgia Laws 1916, No. 539.

Union Pac. R. Co. v. Public Service Commission, 248 U. S. 67, 39 Sup. Ct. 24, 63 L. Ed. 131. Missouri statute.

Flexner v. Farson, 248 U. S. 289, 39 Sup. Ct. 97, 63 L. Ed. 250. Kentucky Civ. Code, § 51, subsec. 6.

Union Tank Line Co. v. Wright, 249 U. S. 275, 39 Sup. Ct. 276, 63 L. Ed. 602. Georgia Civ. Code, §§ 989, 990, 1031.

Standard Oil Co. v. Graves, 249 U. S. 389, 39 Sup. Ct. 320, 63 L. Ed. 662. Washington Laws 1907, c. 192.

Chalker v. Birmingham & N. W. R. Co., 249 U. S. 522, 39 Sup. Ct. 366, 63 L. Ed. 748. Tennessee Laws 1909, c. 479.

a. Northern Pac. Ry. Co. v. North Dakota ex rel. Langer, 250 U. S. 135, 39 Sup. Ct. 502, 63 L. Ed. 897. North Dakota statute.

a. Dakota Cent. Tel. Co. v. South Dakota ex rel. Payne, 250 U. S. 163, 39 Sup. Ct. 507, 63 L. Ed. 910, 4 A. L. R. 1623. South Dakota statute.[18]

Pennsylvania R. Co. v. Public Service Commission, 250 U. S. 566, 40 Sup. Ct. 36, 63 L. Ed. 1142. Pennsylvania Laws 1911, p. 1053, § 7.

a. Postal Telegraph-Cable Co. v. Warren-Godwin Lumber Co., 251 U. S. 27, 40 Sup. Ct. 69, 64 L. Ed. 118. Mississippi statute.[14]

Travis v. Yale & Towne Mfg. Co., 252 U. S. 60, 40 Sup. Ct. 228, 64 L. Ed. 460. New York Laws 1919, c. 627.

---

[18] On the authority of this case, similar statutes of other states were held inoperative in Kansas v. Burleson, 250 U. S. 188, 39 Sup. Ct. 512, 63 L. Ed. 926, Burleson v. Dempcy, 250 U. S. 191, 39 Sup. Ct. 511, 63 L. Ed. 929, and MacLeod v. New England Telephone & Telegraph Co., 250 U. S. 195, 39 Sup. Ct. 511, 63 L. Ed. 934.

[14] On the authority of this case, a similar statute of Indiana was held inoperative in Western Union Tel. Co. v. Boegli, 251 U. S. 315, 40 Sup. Ct. 167, 64 L. Ed. 281.

Oklahoma Operating Co. v. Love, 252 U.
S. 331, 40 Sup. Ct. 338, 64 L. Ed. 596.
Oklahoma Rev. Laws 1910, § 8235.[15]

Kenney v. Supreme Lodge of the World,
Loyal Order of Moose, 252 U. S. 411,
40 Sup. Ct. 371, 64 L. Ed. 638, 10 A. L.
R. 716. Illinois statute.

Askren v. Continental Oil Co., 252 U. S.
444, 40 Sup. Ct. 355, 64 L. Ed. 654.
New Mexico Laws 1919, c. 93, p. 182.

Ward v. Board of Com'rs of Love County, 253 U. S. 17, 40 Sup. Ct. 419, 64 L.
Ed. 751. Oklahoma statute.

Wallace v. Hines, 253 U. S. 66, 40 Sup.
Ct. 435, 64 L. Ed. 782. North Dakota
Laws 1919, c. 222.

Hawke v. Smith, 253 U. S. 221, 253 U. S.
231, 40 Sup. Ct. 498, 64 L. Ed. 877.
Ohio Constitution, amendment of 1918.

Ohio Valley Water Co. v. Ben Avon
Borough, 253 U. S. 287, 40 Sup. Ct.
527, 64 L. Ed. 908. Pennsylvania
Laws 1913, p. 1429, art. 6, § 31.

---

[15] This decision was followed in Oklahoma Gin Co.
v. Oklahoma, 252 U. S. 339, 40 Sup. Ct. 341, 64 L. Ed.
600.

Royster Guano Co. v. Virginia, 253 U. S.
412, 40 Sup. Ct. 560, 64 L. Ed. 989.
Virginia Laws 1916, c. 472.

Johnson v. Maryland, 254 U. S. 51, 41
Sup. Ct. 16, 65 L. Ed. 126. Maryland
Code, art. 56, § 143, as amended by
Laws 1918, c. 85.

Turner v. Wade, 254 U. S. 64, 41 Sup. Ct.
27, 65 L. Ed. 134. Georgia Laws 1913,
p. 123, §§ 6, 7.

Bank of Minden v. Clement, 256 U. S.
126, 41 Sup. Ct. 408, 65 L. Ed. 857.
Louisiana Laws 1914, No. 189.

Bethlehem Motors Corporation v. Flynt,
256 U. S. 421, 41 Sup. Ct. 571, 65 L.
Ed. 1029. North Carolina Laws 1917,
c. 231.

Bowman v. Continental Oil Co., 256 U.
S. 642, 41 Sup. Ct. 606, 65 L. Ed. 1139.
New Mexico Laws 1919, c. 93, p. 182.

Kansas City Southern Ry. v. Road Imp.
Dist. No. 6, of Little River County,
256 U. S. 658, 41 Sup. Ct. 604, 65 L.
Ed. 1151. Arkansas Laws 1915, No.
338.

Eureka Pipe Line Co. v. Hallanan, 257 U. S. 265, 42 Sup. Ct. 101, 66 L. Ed. 227. West Virginia Laws 1919, Ex. Sess. c. 5.[16]

Dahnke-Walker Milling Co. v. Bondurant, 257 U. S. 282, 42 Sup. Ct. 106, 66 L. Ed. 239. Kentucky Stat. 1915, § 571.

---

[16] This ruling was reaffirmed in United Fuel Gas Co. v. Hallanan, 257 U. S. 277, 42 Sup. Ct. 105, 66 L. Ed. 234.

# MUNICIPAL ORDINANCES

## DECLARED UNCONSTITUTIONAL
## BY THE UNITED STATES
## SUPREME COURT

---

Eubank v. Richmond, 226 U. S. 137, 33 Sup. Ct. 76, 57 L. Ed. 156, 42 L. R. A. (N. S.) 1123, Ann. Cas. 1914B, 192.

Williams v. City of Talladega, 226 U. S. 404, 33 Sup. Ct. 116, 57 L. Ed. 275.

New York Cent. & H. R. R. Co. v. Board of Chosen Freeholders of Hudson County, 227 U. S. 248, 33 Sup. Ct. 269, 57 L. Ed. 499 (county ordinance).

Home Telephone & Telegraph Co. v. Los Angeles, 227 U. S. 278, 33 Sup. Ct. 312, 57 L. Ed. 510.

Grand Trunk Western R. Co. v. South Bend, 227 U. S. 544, 33 Sup. Ct. 303, 57 L. Ed. 633, 44 L. R. A. (N. S.) 405.

Owensboro v. Cumberland Telephone & Telegraph Co., 230 U. S. 58, 33 Sup. Ct. 988, 57 L. Ed. 1389.

Boise Artesian Hot & Cold Water Co. v. Boise City, 230 U. S. 84, 33 Sup. Ct. 997, 57 L. Ed. 1400.

Old Colony Trust Co. v. Omaha, 230 U. S. 100, 33 Sup. Ct. 967, 57 L. Ed. 1410.

Adams Express Co. v. New York, 232 U. S. 14, 34 Sup. Ct. 203, 58 L. Ed. 483.

United States Express Co. v. New York, 232 U. S. 35, 34 Sup. Ct. 209, 58 L. Ed. 492 (same ordinance as 232 U. S. 14, 34 Sup. Ct. 203, 58 L. Ed. 483).

Russell v. Sebastian, 233 U. S. 195, 34 Sup. Ct. 517, 58 L. Ed. 912, L. R. A. 1918E, 882, Ann. Cas. 1914C, 1282.

Sault Ste. Marie v. International Transit Co., 234 U. S. 333, 34 Sup. Ct. 826, 58 L. Ed. 1337, 52 L. R. A. (N. S.) 574.

Gast Realty & Investment Co. v. Schneider Granite Co., 240 U. S. 55, 36 Sup. Ct. 254, 60 L. Ed. 523.

Buchanan v. Warley, 245 U. S. 60, 38 Sup.
Ct. 16, 62 L. Ed. 149, L. R. A. 1918C, 210,
Ann. Cas. 1918A, 1201.

Denver v. Denver Union Water Co., 246 U.
S. 178, 38 Sup. Ct. 278, 62 L. Ed. 649.

Covington v. South Covington & C. St. Ry.
Co., 246 U. S. 413, 38 Sup. Ct. 376, 62 L.
Ed. 802.

Detroit United R. Co. v. Detroit, 248 U. S.
429, 39 Sup. Ct. 151, 63 L. Ed. 341.

Lincoln Gas & Electric Light Co. v. Lincoln,
250 U. S. 256, 39 Sup. Ct. 454, 63 L. Ed.
968 (void under state Constitution).

Los Angeles v. Los Angeles Gas & Electric
Corporation, 251 U. S. 32, 40 Sup. Ct. 76,
64 L. Ed. 121.

# ACTS OF COMMISSIONS,

## OR SIMILAR BODIES ACTING UNDER LEGISLATIVE AUTHORITY, DECLARED UNCONSTITUTIONAL BY THE UNITED STATES SUPREME COURT

Oregon R. & N. Co. v. Fairchild, 224 U. S. 510, 32 Sup. 535, 56 L. Ed. 863.

Ohio Railroad Commission v. Worthington, 225 U. S. 101, 32 Sup. Ct. 653, 56 L. Ed. 1004.

Yazoo & M. V. R. Co. v. Greenwood Grocery Co., 227 U. S. 1, 33 Sup. Ct. 213, 57 L. Ed. 389.

Minnesota Rate Cases, 230 U. S. 352, 33 Sup. Ct. 729, 57 L. Ed. 1511, 48 L. R. A. (N. S.) 1151, Ann. Cas. 1916A, 18 (as to certain railroad).

Missouri Rate Cases, 230 U. S. 474, 33 Sup. Ct. 975, 57 L. Ed. 1571 (as to certain railroad).

Houston E. & W. T. Ry. Co. v. United States, 234 U. S. 342, 34 Sup. Ct. 833, 58 L. Ed. 1341.

Illinois Cent. R. Co. v. Louisiana Railroad Commission, 236 U. S. 157, 35 Sup. Ct. 275, 59 L. Ed. 517.

Myles Salt Co. v. Board of Com'rs of Iberia & St. Mary Drainage Dist., 239 U. S. 478, 36 Sup. Ct. 204, 60 L. Ed. 392, L. R. A. 1918E, 190.

Greene v. Louisville & I. R. Co., 244 U. S 499, 37 Sup. Ct. 673, 61 L. Ed. 1280, Ann. Cas. 1917E, 88 (invalid under state Constitution).

Louisville & N. R. Co. v. Greene, 244 U. S. 522, 37 Sup. Ct. 683, 61 L. Ed. 1291, Ann. Cas. 1917E, 97.

Northern Ohio Traction & Light Co. v. Ohio ex rel. Pontius, 245 U. S. 574, 38 Sup. Ct. 196, 62 L. Ed. 481, L. R. A. 1918E, 865.

Western Union Tel. Co. v. Foster, 247 U. S. 105, 38 Sup. Ct. 438, 62 L. Ed. 1006, 1 A. L. R. 1278.

Brooks-Scanlon Co. v. Railroad Commission of Louisiana, 251 U. S. 396, 40 Sup. Ct. 183, 64 L. Ed. 323.

Great Northern R. Co. v. Cahill, 253 U. S. 71, 40 Sup. Ct. 457, 64 L. Ed. 787, 10 A. L. R. 1335.

Vandalia R. Co. v. Schnull, 255 U. S. 113, 41 Sup. Ct. 324, 65 L. Ed. 539.

*

# INDEX

[ 175 ]

# INDEX

[ 176 ]

# INDEX

# INDEX

# INDEX

# INDEX

[The figures refer to pages]

†